Piagetian Research

Volume Seven

PIAGETIAN RESEARCH:
Compilation and Commentary

Volume Seven

Training Techniques

Sohan Modgil, PhD and Celia Modgil, MPhil

Foreword by Professor Bärbel Inhelder
The University of Geneva

NFER Publishing Company Ltd

1116

Published by the NFER Publishing Company Ltd.,
2 Jennings Buildings, Thames Avenue,
Windsor, Berks. SL4 1QS
Registered Office: The Mere, Upton Park, Slough, Berks., SL1 2DQ
First published 1976
© Sohan and Celia Modgil, 1976
ISBN 0 85633 107 4

Printed in Great Britain by
Staples Printers, Rochester, Kent.
Distributed in the USA by Humanities Press Inc.,
Atlantic Highlands, New Jersey 07716 USA.

Contents

To Gita and Ramayana

With Love

FOREWORD

I most sincerely thank Dr Sohan and Celia Modgil for asking me to write a foreword to the series of eight volumes which they are at present compiling. We all know the interest that was shown in, and the success of, the previous book, *Piagetian Research: A Handbook of Recent Studies*. Now, two years later, eight follow-up volumes are being published. We are well aware of what this represents in terms of continuity and devotion to such a long-term task.

The rapid extension of Piaget-inspired research is very impressive; in this series 3700 references are mentioned. It would seem that such an extension is explained by the need for a general theory in fundamental psychology. Another possible explanation is the growing awareness of the gaps in strictly behaviourist theory, on the one hand, and on the other, the continued emergence of new applications for the work carried out in Geneva in the fields of education and psychopathology. Recent studies confirm this trend.

Pleasing though this extension is, however, we are somewhat disturbed by the fact that the replication of our experiments does not always show a sufficient understanding of Piagetian theory on the part of the authors of these new works. We are of course the first to admit that such understanding is not easy to acquire, especially since this form of psychology is closely linked to a certain form of epistemology. Once understood, this form of epistemology appears to be that which best suits genetic psychology, as both are essentially constructivist. Constructivism implies that knowledge is not acquired merely under the impact of empirical experience, as suggested by behaviourist theory, although of course such impact is not entirely excluded from the process. It is also opposed to innate theory, to which, it seems, recourse is frequently had today (maturation being a factor which intervenes, but not exclusively). Constructivism emphasizes the child's or the subject's activity during the course of cognitive development: in other words, everything derives from actions and is eventually translated into coherent and logical thought operations.

In order to promote the necessary understanding, Sohan and Celia Modgil have systematically encouraged the reader to return to the original texts. If authors who have an excellent knowledge of the work of Piaget and his colleagues slightly misunderstand our theoretical position — which is in no way maturationist but rather epigenetic — one can easily imagine the misunderstanding of researchers who are less well informed and further away from Geneva. It is one thing to recognize the necessary sequence of the stages, but another thing altogether to explain them by invoking an innate 'programme'. Piaget's explanation, which is best presented in constructivist terms, deals with the sequence of stages by a process of equilibration or autoregulation. This regulatory activity enables the subject truly to construct knowledge – something which simple maturation does not do.

This point of view is fundamental to the understanding of Piagetian psychology; but more than that, it seems to us to constitute a particularly useful approach to questions of educational application since this form of autoconstruction corresponds more than any other perspective to the ideal called 'the active school', an ideal rarely carried out in practice.

In a constructivist perspective of this kind, it is clearly the sequence of stages which is important and not the chronological ages; the latter vary considerably from one environment to another and also depend on the experimental procedures being used. It is not astonishing that Bryant obtains convservation responses at earlier ages than those noted by us: we ourselves have obtained notable accelerations using operatory learning procedures developed in collaboration with H. Sinclair and M. Bovet (1974). We have recently published the results of a study (Inhelder *et al.*, 1975) which show stable acquisition of conservation notions as of age 5 if the following procedure is used: rather than merely deforming an object such as a ball of clay or modifying a collection of discrete elements, one removes part of or an element of the object(s) and moves it to another spot. In this case conservation appears earlier because the child understands two things he did not grasp during the simple deformations: firstly, that changes in shape are the result of displacements, and secondly, that in the course of these displacements what appears at the end is identical to what was removed at the start (this is what Piaget calls 'commutability'). We highlight this piece of work in order to show the much lesser importance of chronological age which can so easily be accelerated or delayed according to circumstances. The main point is the mode of construction which obeys constant laws and this characteristic is best exemplified by constructivism as we have defined it earlier.

We would also like to add that the recent discoveries of T. Bower and others concerning the innateness of certain behaviours which Piaget had not observed at the sensorimotor level do not contradict constructivism, since these primitive reactions do not directly result in higher-order behaviours but are reconstructed on different levels. These reconstructions are themselves not innate, but evidence of the constructive activities we have already observed elsewhere.

I should like to congratulate Dr Sohan and Celia Modgil on their fine effort in bringing together in these eight volumes the numerous pieces of work, thus rendering them accessible to researchers. We sincerely hope that this will encourage further progress in genetic psychology and all its applications.

Bärbel Inhelder,
University of Geneva

PREFACE

The eight volumes in the present series, *Piagetian Research*, together with the previous publication, *Piagetian Research: A Handbook of Recent Studies*, 1974, are intended to serve a wide range of needs for both teacher and learner at all levels: for university and college lecturers; post-graduate research students; those training to be educational psychologists; teachers and others following a wide range of advanced diploma courses; and education and psychology students at undergraduate level, following Educational and Developmental Psychology options. Research projects have been included which have implications for psychiatrists, paediatricians, rehabilitation and social workers.

In one sense, there are many authors to these volumes. The research evidence included is dependent on the countless efforts of Piaget's followers. In fairness, our gratitude is extended to those followers whose researches contribute immeasurably to the contents of these volumes. In particular, we acknowledge the cooperation of the many researchers personally communicating and forwarding papers for inclusion. Some collaborators have contributed material previously unpublished. These contributions, together with their accompanying correspondence, have resulted in a more comprehensive output.

We owe a very special debt of gratitude to Geneva University, and to universities here and abroad. Likewise, the inspiration of Professors Piaget and Inhelder, together with the general support of Professor Ruth Beard, Dr Gordon Cross, and Professor Marcel Goldschmid, are acknowledged.

It is an honour to have received such distinguished recognition for the volumes from Professor Bärbel Inhelder's gracious Foreword. We offer sincere thanks and gratitude for her interest and involvement and for the pleasant meeting in Geneva.

Enver Carim, an author in his own right as well as a perceptive editor, has provided the expertise necessary for such an ambitious series. Further to these more direct qualities Enver Carim has a profound philosophy with respect to a number of areas of knowledge including psychology and unusual drive and energy. We are indebted to him for all his support and acknowledge with gratitude the tremendous contributions he has made to this series.

Sohan Modgil
Celia Modgil
July 1976

INTRODUCTION

The eight volumes in the present series *Piagetian Research* together with the previous publication *Piagetian Research: A Handbook of Recent Studies*, 1974, are designed to make available a substantial number of Piaget-oriented researches that may be useful for immediate information as well as for long-term reference. The accelerating expansion of Piagetian research has led to an acute need for a source book more comprehensive than the ordinary textbook but more focused than the scattered periodical literature. More specifically, it should give the reader access to source materials that elaborate upon most Piagetian topics. Likewise, such volumes should offer students examples of a variety of approaches utilized by researchers in their efforts to investigate cognitive development. The numerous researches assembled present experimental subjects whose chronological ages range from birth to 98 years. The intended readership is therefore broad, from those interested in the very young, in adolescents, in the elderly.

The present volumes, as well as recording the replications and extensions of Piaget's work, include reflections on, speculations about, and analyses of the various problems of the theory. Hopefully, this should in turn provide inspiration for further elaboration, extension and revision. The research worker is provided with a broad spectrum of original sources from which an appreciation in depth of the theoretical, methodological and practical questions relevant to a Piagetian framework can be obtained. While it is conceded that a secondary source is not the ideal way to comprehend the theory, nevertheless it can provide the reader with a basic direction to the problem at hand.

The material gathered has been heavily drawn from University degree theses, published and unpublished researches up to and as recent as July 1976.* It became apparent that the subject matter was voluminous and that there were many ways to subdivide the Piagetian cognitive researches. In choosing the articles, the criteria were made as

---

* The authors have been alert to studies appearing up to August 1976 (after the completion of the main manuscript) and brief details of further selected researches have been added in order to enrich particular areas of inquiry and discussion. Hopefully, researches within this category will receive full treatment in anticipated follow-up volumes.

objective as possible, while recognizing that a personal slant is bound to influence the selection. Despite an extensive search it is not unlikely that valuable articles have been overlooked. To these researchers apologies are extended. In assembling these researches the principal objective was to include only those which satisfy one of the following criteria: Piaget-oriented (replications or extensions); developmental in nature; or those which have discussed their findings within the Piagetian framework.

The tables of content reflect a broad range of studies, and represent most of the major subdivisions of Piagetian literature. It must be pointed out that while some articles fall naturally into certain specific volumes, others would have fitted simultaneously into more than one volume, this being in part due to the inability to distinguish between the analytic and synthetic. Consequently, it was difficult to select one single scheme that would satisfy all readers and many arbitrary decisions had to be made. There is obviously considerable reliance on the use of cross references.

The compilation covers fifteen areas, assembled in eight volumes — each volume focuses on one/two major aspects of Piaget's work. The main areas covered are: Piaget's Cognitive Theory and his major works, Sensorimotor Intelligence, Conservation, Training Techniques, Logic, Space, Handicapped Children, Cross-Cultural Research, The School Curriculum, Morality, Socialization, Test Development, Animism, Imagery and Memory.

Each volume consists of an integrated review of the range of recent studies followed by abstracts of these researches arranged, in the main, alphabetically. Where details of early research are essential to illustrate the evolution of a particular area of study, these are not represented by a full abstract, but are included in the introductory review. Although many cross references to related abstracts are included, the reviews preceding the abstracts are not intended to be fully critical of the validity and reliability of experimental design. This is partly due to the fact that, unless full details are available (sometimes these have neither been published fully, nor the definition of concepts made meaningful), this would be inimical, and partly because the amount of work involved in a critical evaluation of every study in a work of this breadth would be prohibitive.

In comparison to most publications, an unusual amount of detail of researches is made available, and to accompany this with an equal amount of discussion, although essential, could introduce complexity in the aims of the volumes. Some of the abstracts (indicated by an asterisk) have been written by the authors themselves and reproduced in their entirety. It is realized that some abstracts are of only marginal importance, yet their inclusion is essential to show general developmental patterns.

It is the authors' intention that the reader, having investigated the range of available material, would then consult the original research according to his specific interests. Advanced research depends a great deal on what sources and data are available for study, and there is a consequent tendency for some parts of the field to be ploughed over and over again, while others remain virtually untouched.

The list of references included at the end of each volume together form a comprehensive bibliography encompassing over 3,500 references. Volume One additionally includes a comprehensive survey of Piaget's works, arranged chronologically.

Every care has been taken to report the results of the researches as accurately as possible — any misinterpretation of the results is accidental. It must be conceded that all the studies included do not receive equal coverage. While the overall response to the circulated requests was excellent, some shortcomings in the volumes are due partly to some failure of response. While deficiencies of the final product are our own responsibility, they exist in spite of a number of advisers who gave their time generously.

Training Techniques

a. Introduction

Although training may serve to accelerate concept acquisition, most supporters of Piaget would argue that it is impossible to alter the sequence or bring about too rapid a change. For example, Freeberg and Payne (1965, p. 80) focus on Bruner's (1960) position in that 'almost any subject matter, if properly organized can be taught at the pre-school level. . . . At somewhat the other extreme is the essentially maturational position of Inhelder and Piaget (1958) who argue for specific levels of cognitive development that must be achieved before certain conceptual strategies can be learned (e.g. those basic to inductive reasoning)'. Freeberg and Payne further draw attention to Ausubel who would also doubt the likelihood of inducing certain concepts at the 'pre-operational' stage in Piaget's system. However, he looks upon these conceptual stages as 'nothing more than approximations' that are 'susceptible to environmental influences' (Ausubel, 1965, pp. 11–12).

Piaget (1964) has discussed three criteria as vital in ascertaining whether a researcher has '. . . succeeded in teaching operational structures' (p. 17). The first is the durability of learning. Some studies have demonstrated that provoked conservation could be sustained three weeks to six months after training (Fournier, 1967; Gelman, 1967; Goldschmid, 1968a). Goldschmid (1969) concludes that '. . . it is indeed possible to accelerate the long-lasting acquisition of certain Piagetian concepts'. However, other researchers do not agree with Goldschmid. Lovell (1969) maintains 'the evidence, . . . as to whether training on conservation leads to improvement on performance in respect to seriation, classification etc., is only meaningful if the relevant schemata are related in a general structure. If they are not, then these involve independently learned skills. . . Piagetian test items have no more and no less rationale than those employed in the Binet scales — namely, they are tasks which children at certain ages can perform. While, then there is evidence that training can induce a cognitive schema, which has durability and at best limited transfer, the evidence is still — and Goldschmid himself admits to this — not at all clear as to whether there is a change in the operational structure in a strictly Piagetian sense . . . . Training which generates these rather narrow schemas at first may well be advantageous to the child. Operative thought may be extended to other areas earlier, but this I don't know'. He agrees with Goldschmid concerning the need for longitudinal studies of children who have experienced training and would like training to be extended to such concepts as time, temperature and space.

The second criterion postulated by Piaget (1964) concerns the vital issue of generalization or transfer to related cognitive strategies. The studies of Fournier (1967), Gelman (1967) and Goldschmid (1968a) have shown training to enhance the acquisition of conservation concepts with varied degrees of transfer to related and hierarchical concepts and sub-concepts. In Goldschmid's study (1969, *op. cit.*) two types of transfer tests — Scales A and B (Goldschmid and Bentler, 1968a; 1968b) included six tasks which were intercorrelated and homogeneous. The training involved three of these tasks. Post-tests demonstrated that performance improved significantly not only on the trained tasks but on all six tasks of the scales. A more remote transfer also occurred to another dimension of conservation as measured by Scale C. However, the study has encountered many criticisms (Lovell, 1969; Inhelder, 1969; Beilin, 1969; and Elkind, 1969).

Piaget's third criterion is best described in his own words: 'In the case of each learning experience what was the operational level of the subject before the experience and what more complex structures has this subject succeeded in learning? . . . We must look at each specific learning experience from the point of view of the spontaneous operations which were present at the outset and the operational level which has been achieved after the learning experience' (Piaget, 1964).

Another criterion is formulated by Smedslund (1961) as 'the resistance to extinction'. In an experiment designed to induce conservation of weight he found that children who were operational on conservation after training tended to extinguish their conservation behaviour when the examiner surreptitiously removed some clay from one of the two objects. Whereas another group of children, who were operational on conservation spontaneously, tended to resist extinction. Goldschmid (1969) employed the same extinction test as Smedslund for weight (1961b) and casts doubt on Smedslund's findings, whereas Kohnstamm (1966) has suggested that if he were to apply this criterion of extinction, he would only do so '. . . after having accustomed the young child to the idea that the stranger (E) sometimes systematically tries to mislead him, otherwise the timid child may fall back on the old answer which E definitely suggests to be correct, while the self-confident child may resist. Variables of personality or child–adult interaction should not interfere with the testing for quality of cognitive growth' (p. 63). Two other critics of Smedslund's (1961b) study concerning conservation and resistance to extinction are Hall and Simpson (1968). They argued that this study has had to '. . . bear a very heavy empirical and theoretical burden'. Hall and Simpson agreed that conservation can be extinguished, drawing on the results of several extinction studies of their own. They proposed a learning explanation for the development and extinction of conservation. However, Smedslund (1968) comments briefly on the theoretical issues involved and on Hall's and Simpson's failure to replicate his findings. 'I still believe that the findings of my original pilot study can be replicated . . . However, a replication would seem to require a very careful balancing of emphasis on standardization of procedures and consideration of the subtleties of the experimenter–child interaction.' Moreover, he maintained that conservation can never be extinguished, since a defining property of true conservation is that it is logically necessary and therefore unextinguishable.

In an article entitled, 'Extinction of conservation: a methodological and theoretical analysis', Miller (1971) drew attention to the recent exchange in the *Merrill-Palmer Quarterly* (Hall and Simpson, 1968; Smedslund, 1968) which was directed to the question of whether the Piagetian concept of conservation was subject to experimental extinction. In Miller's exchange a vital theoretical question was raised: 'Is conservation an empirically learned and therefore extinguishable response (Hall and Simpson), or is it rather a logically necessary product of the development of concrete operations (Smedslund–Piaget)?', p. 319. Miller attempted to clarify some of the issues involved in the Hall and Simpson–Smedslund debate. Results from selected studies are briefly reviewed with a critical analysis of the methodological and conceptual problems present in extinction research. (Details appear later.)

Contradiction, surprise, and cognitive change: the effects of disconfirmation of belief on conservers and non-conservers was investigated by Miller (1973) in non-conservers (mean CA = eight years four months), young conservers (mean CA = eight years 10 months), and older conservers (mean CA = 11 years). The results demonstrated that observable surprise proved infrequent in all Ss. 'In contrast, changes in conservation judgment were frequent, although the degree of change was reduced somewhat if an appropriate explanation was required. The three groups were generally indistinguishable in the extent to which they changed. Evidence of active resistance to change . . . was absent in non-conservers but appeared in about half the conservers. Older conservers were no more likely to resist extinction than were younger conservers', p. 47. (Details of the study appear later.) Miller maintains, 'This study produced more evidence of resistance to extinction than had the majority of previous studies. Thus, in three studies Hall and his associates (Hall and Kingsley, 1968; Hall and Simpson, 1968; Kingsley and Hall, 1967) found that only 10 of 92 conservers were able to resist extinction by uttering an explanation which denied the validity of the non-conservation outcome. In this study 22 of 41 conservers produced such explanations. Similarly, both Hall and Simpson (1968) and Smith (1968) reported that conservers would readily switch to non-conservation predictions following an extinction experience. The present study, however, found that only 66 per cent of such changed predictions were accompanied by typical non-conservation explanations. In both cases, apparent extinction proves at least somewhat deceptive upon closer examination', p. 60.

With respect to Miller studies (*op. cit.*), Miller and Brownell (1975) argued, '. . . there are methodological limitations in the research conducted thus far. Most of the studies have focused on conservation of weight, thus making conclusions about conservation in general uncertain. And in both the extinction and the surprise paradigms, the social pressures from an adult tester may well have obscured any feelings of certainty that the child possessed,' p. 992. (The Miller and Brownell study is described, more appropriately in Volume Five, in the present series, *Piagetian Research*.)

To determine whether children would relinquish their belief in Piagetian concepts upon presentation of disconfirming evidence, Miller and Lipps (1973) administered tasks of conservation of weight and transitivity of weight to subjects from third, fourth and sixth grade. '. . . the discrepant feedback consisted of three trials with either non-conservation or non-transitivity outcomes. Resistance or extinction was inferred from the S's explanations for the outcomes, his responses on subsequent trials, and his performance on a one-month delayed post-test. Conservation Ss showed only moderate resistance by any of these measures. Transitivity Ss were much less likely than conservers to change their judgments on either the initial or the delayed test; they also showed the expected developmental increase in resistance to extinction', Miller and Lipps (*op. cit*).

An attempt to extinguish conservation of weight in college students was made by Miller, Schwartz, and Stewart (1973) in 18 male and 18 female undergraduates with a median age of 20 years one month. A pre-test for conservation of weight showed that all S's were fully operational. This was succeeded by three similar problems on which feedback was provided following the subject's judgment and explanation. 'The feedback in each case indicated non-conservation. The S was asked to explain the outcomes; questioning continued until he either appeared satisfied with an answer or was unable to provide anything further. The session concluded with two post-test trials without feedback. Two main measures of change were examined. One was the subject's explanations for the outcomes. Of particular interest were denials that non-conservation had occurred . . . The other main index of change was response to subsequent conservation trials. There were 42 non-conservation judgments on the four trials following the first feedback, an average of slightly more than one per subject. Males and females did not differ in their tendency to give non-conservation answers. Twenty-two of the 36 Ss never gave a non-conservation judgment. In addition, only one S who switched to non-conservation offered the perceptual explanation of the typical non-conserver. Most of the non-conservation judgments were accompanied by considerably more sophisticated explanations', p. 316. (Details follow.)

Chiseri (1975) argued, 'The findings of Hall and Kingsley are not consistent with the results of a study of Miller, Schwartz, and Stewart (1973) where 72 per cent of 36 college students resisted on a first extinction trial, and for two subsequent extinction trials and post-tests, 60 per cent never gave a non-conservation response. In Miller *et al.*, a peer experimenter was used and ample provision made for the subjects to reflect upon and express their explanations. A direct comparison of the two studies is somewhat inappropriate due to the vast procedural differences and, in any case, it still remains to account for the notably high extinction rate reported by Hall and Kingsley. Prior to the extinction trial, Hall and Kingsley had each subject fill in a "table" . . . on the conservation status of weight and mass under various changes of other qualifiers of an object. Subjects who wrote that weight "conserves" under changes of shape were deemed to have correctly responded to the pertinent part of the questionnaire. In empirical fact, however, even the shape transformation can result in a change of weight through the phenomenon of sublimation. The rate of exchange of material between a solid and the surrounding medium is proportional to its surface area, and changing its shape (i.e., surface area to volume ratio) will cause an accelerated rate of sublimation and consequent loss of weight, and its detection would depend on the sensitivity of the scale employed. A further complication in responding to the table is that mass is an abstract construct and essentially unmeasurable (Jammer, 1961), its conservation being dependent upon adherence to a theory of matter', pp. 139—140. Chiseri was therefore intent to test the hypothesis that the conservation questionnaire would render college students more amenable to an unexpected instance of non-conservation of weight, and thus likely to resist extinction. Fifty-four university psychology students comprised the sample. The results showed that adults, if permitted sufficient latitude and not 'intimidated by technicalities of content, will sustain a conservation hypothesis in extinction paradigms'. (Details are given later.)

More recently, Strauss (1974) argued, 'This type of study was, however, . . . conducted (Strauss, Danziger and Ramati, 1974) with college students, and it was found that none gave up laws of weight and matter conservation or gravity. Of the 70 per cent of those who accepted the nonbalancing phenomenon, all explained it in terms of the laws of the lever. This data calls into question a number of "extinction" studies since all of the experimenters understood implicitly and explicitly that they were tapping Ss' notions of weight conservation alone. Further research of this type is necessary, and, if the above conclusions are sustained, we would then have an answer to Brainerd's query about how it could be that trained conservers of weight are no less resistant to "extinction" procedures than natural weight conservers', p. 179.

Brainerd (1973) considered the varied criteria as either unnecessary or inappropriate. He argued that explanations were in fact inappropriate criteria for assessing the presence of cognitive structures. He maintained that some subset of subjects may actually possess the cognitive operation(s) being assessed but fail a test that demands their expression in language — drawing on Piaget's assertion that language is dependent on operativity such that a cognitive operation may develop prior to the individual's being able to express that operation in language with the reverse never occuring. He claimed that the preferred criterion for assessing cognitive structures, is a subject's simple dichotomous choice, e.g., yes—no or same—different. He asserted, that such a criterion was not subject to any known source of error. In a Paper entitled, 'Neo-Piagetian training experiments revisited: Is there any support for the cognitive-developmental stage hypothesis?', Brainerd with reference to Strauss' (1972) three categories of stage-related training experiments draws attention as follows: 'Training treatments which introduce disequilibrium into the cognitive system from external sources have proved fruitful means of inducing concrete-operational concepts . . . Ss who evidence a given concrete-operational concept on the pre-tests tend to be more susceptible to training experiences designed to induce that concept than Ss who do not evidence the concept on the pre-test . . . Training treatments that may be interpreted as focusing narrowly on a single conservation — relevant operation . . . have successfully induced conservation concepts . . . If we have two concrete-operational concepts A and B such that A invariably precedes B during the course of normal cognitive growth, A probably will prove easier to train than B in Ss who possess neither concept . . . there is no definitive evidence that multiple operations treatments will induce conservation . . . The resistance of conservation concepts to extinction

treatments is neither universally low nor universally high ...
appreciable differences in the extinction resistance of trained and
natural conservers have not been observed', p. 366. (Details appear
later.)

Strauss (1974) replies to Brainerd's (1973) review in which the latter
criticized the former's (1972) article entitled, 'Inducing cognitive
development and learning: a review of short-term training experiments
I: the organismic-developmental approach'. The 30 page reply includes
such headings and sub-headings as: the criterion problem; training
experiments; disequilibrium; adaptational disequilibrium; organizational
disequilibrium; mental operations; training individual operations;
training multiple operations; and extinction studies. A summary of the
reply appears later.

Likewise, Kuhn (1974) has argued, 'Brainerd's (1973) discussion
rested on a critical unexamined assumption. This assumption is that for
any given cognitive operation(s), a method of assessment can in
actuality be devised that both unambiguously assesses the presence or
absence of those operations and entails nothing more from the subject
than a choice between two alternatives (e.g., same versus different).
Any dichotomous choice method, in fact, is subject to the equally, if
not more, troubling probability of Type 1 errors. Some Ss, in other
words, may make the appropriate choice for idiosyncratic or
extraneous reasons and be assessed as possessing the operation(s) in
question when they in truth do not possess it. In the context of a
training study, this source of error becomes critical. If either training or
assessment itself provides the S with any cues that enable him to make
correctly the requisite two-choice discrimination, he is likely to "pass"
the post-test, though his basis for the choice is irrelevant to the
concepts or operations being assessed. As Brainerd (1973) noted,
stimulus refinements can gradually eliminate many such cues, reducing
the probability of "false positive" responses ... All dichotomous
choice methods devised to date, however, fall far short of having
eliminated all possibilities of false positive responses. More fundamen-
tally, whether methodological improvements alone can ever lead to an
accomplishment of the objective is debatable. If a subject does nothing
more than choose between two alternatives presented by the E, can the
judgment that underlies his choice ever be known for sure? Overall, the
generalization seems warranted that the most trustworthy methods for
assessing the attainment of a given cognitive structure are those that
elicit a variety of responses, both verbal and nonverbal, and make an
inference based on this constellation of responses', pp. 591—592.

If a trained conserver has genuinely attained conservation, his
explanations ought to closely resemble those given by natural
conservers. Kuhn (1974) has pointed the critical problem in the use of

appropriate explanations as a criterion. 'Most training methods . . .
entail as part of the training some presentation of conservation
explanations either implicitly or in the form of explicit verbal rules.
Thus, conservation explanations cannot retain their status as indexes of
the understanding of the principle of conservation in post-training
assessment . . . Thus, once a S has been exposed to such a procedure,
his mention of the possibility of rearrangements during a post-test can
no longer be considered a reflection of his understanding of the
principle of conservation in the way it might in the case of a natural
conserver. Appropriate explanations, then, may be considered as a
necessary but not a sufficient criterion to permit a judgment of genuine
change', p. 592.

Focusing on the 'duration' criterion training studies Kuhn (*op. cit.*)
draws attention to the typical assessment strategy which is to present
one or more additional post-tests some period of time after the initial
post-test. '. . . a subject might during a second post-test a week or
month later make the same responses he did during the first post-test
because (a) he had interpreted those responses as the desired or correct
ones for that situation (*cf.* Kuhn, 1973) and (b) he found himself in the
situation a second time. All this might conceivably occur in the absence
of any understanding of conservation on the S's part. Like the
explanation criterion, then, the duration criterion should be considered
as necessary but not sufficient', p. 592.

The generalization criterion, from a more theoretical viewpoint, is
intricately tied to Piaget's 'structured whole' concept of development.
'If, as Piaget suggested, development consists of a series of major
transformations in the organization of an individual's cognitive
operations, the attainment of a given stage . . . should be marked by a
whole constellation of behavioural acquisitions. Thus, the presence of
other nontrained concrete operational behaviours should be the critical
indicator of whether a trained S has actually reached a concrete
operational level of development . . . however, . . . all of the behaviours
thought to reflect Piaget's stage of concrete operations do not emerge
synchronously (Pinard and Laurendeau, 1969). The various conservations . . . emerge only gradually over a period of several years . . .
The limiting case of such a claim is represented in a theoretical position
like Gagné's (1965, 1968). In Gagné's view, conservation represents the
end point in a long sequence of skills, rules, and concepts, which a child
progressively masters. Hence, Gagné would view the entire criterion of
generalization an unreasonable one . . . If conservation does reflect
some kind of cognitive reorganization, . . . the critical question in the
assessment of training interventions becomes this: How much
generalization to nontrained items is necessary to infer genuine
structural change? There has been no satisfactory answer to this

question. Thus, for every investigator who pronounces his study a success, another investigator may point to any absences of generalization and claim that Ss did not really attain the concept. Until the generalization question is satisfactorily answered, then, pronouncing any given training study a success remains equivocal', (*ibid.*, p. 593).

b. Number

Whiteman and Peisach (1970) draw attention to the fact that researchers like Kingsley and Hall (1967) and Sigel (1966) demonstrate that a combination of training procedures facilitates conservation behaviour. That reversibility training may be more successful when presented as a sensorimotor rather than as a perceptual experience has been demonstrated by Greenfield (1966); and Sonstroem (1966) examined the training effects of combinations of three variables on the conservation of solids: motoric manipulation, screening, and labeling of compensatory attributes. He found that a combination of labeling the physical attributes that changed in a conservation of continuous quantity task and motoric reversibility experience in the same task was the most effective of a number of training procedures in inducing non-operational children to operativity. Whiteman and Peisach administered number and substance tasks incorporating perceptual cues and sensorimotor experience to compensate for the absence of such underlying cognitive schemata as compensation, atomism and reversibility among children of low socioeconomic status. The authors maintain that sensorimotor cues are of relatively greater help to younger children closer to the sensorimotor stages, while perceptual cues are of more aid to older children. The results also demonstrated that 'the situational supports were compensatory for cognitive inadequacies only on the number conservation items, the older children improving on both judgement and explained judgement scores, the younger children only on the judgement score'.

To identify conditions that facilitate conservation of number in 64 three-, four-, and five-year-old children, Miller, Heldmeyer and Miller (1975) administered seven trials of conservation of number varied in the number and type of perceptual supports. The authors argued that it was inaccurate to label young children simply conservers or non-conservers. The majority of the Ss in their study were operational under some conditions and non-operational under others. Perceptual supports, when provided, 'a rudimentary understanding of conservation is revealed. However, the concept is so fragile that it does not appear under usual testing conditions', p. 253. (Details follow.)

Wallach, Wall and Anderson (1967) were intent to determine the nature of training necessary for the inducement of the conservation of number. Wallach and Sprott (1964) indicated that 'conservation under operations that remove defining attributes could be induced through experience with reversibility of these operations'. However, Wohlwill and Lowe (1962) and Smedslund (1962), proposed that experience with addition and subtraction may be critical for conservation. The results of Wallach *et al.* indicated that reversibility training was effective in the inducement of number and that such a training did not need to be accompanied by experience with the act of addition/subtraction. Further, in the absence of reversibility training, training in addition/subtraction by itself did not prove successful in facilitating the acquisition of number conservation. However, certain reservations were suggested by the authors (full details of which are given in Modgil, 1974, pp. 83–84). Roll (1970) further investigated the effect of training in reversibility on the conservation of number. He concludes that the training resulted in a significant increase in conservation response but not in increased verbalization of conservation principles (details are given in Modgil, 1974, pp. 93-94). Strauss (1974) states that in Roll's study, '. . . during one month's time, 16 Ss were administered 44 trials of reversible deformations. Of these 16 Ss, 11 produced conservation judgments on the post-test, but only four were able to justify their judgments. At this point, the criterion problem looms large since if we accept the judgments — only criterion, 69 per cent of the Ss conserved as opposed to only 25 per cent post-test conservers if we accept the judgments—plus—explanations criterion . . . it is not common to find judgments and justifications at different levels, yet in the study 44 per cent of the Ss produced this discrepancy. A second finding, which might also call the assessment procedure into question, was that the age range for Ss who were non-conservers for discontinuous quantity was 5, 7 to 7, 11. This concept is usually acquired naturally around age five. Roll described a second training procedure which was conducted with children who were assessed as intuitive for the same concept and whose age range was from 5, 9 to 8, 1. The findings from the Roll study when taken together seem to show that if relatively older Ss are administered a large number (44) of reversible deformation trials . . . over a long period of time, . . . 43 per cent will be able to argue on a post-test that, when deformed, the objects in the rows are equivalent in number but that only ¼ can explain why this should be the case', p. 172.

The method (explicit reinforcement) consists of giving the S information ('right' or 'wrong' depending on whether the particular transformation preserves quantity or does not) about each of his responses, sometimes accompanied by tangible rewards for correct responses (Wohlwill and Lowe, 1962). In Wohlwill and Lowe's study, in the Reinforced Practice condition two rows of objects equal in length and number were administered. The S was questioned about their relative magnitude. Then the lengths of the rows were made unequal, and the child was questioned again and given feedback. If the child was non-operational he was required to count the sets. If he were operational he was given a token. In the Addition/Subtraction training a non-number-conserving transformation was likewise employed. Objects were removed or added on 2/3 of the trials. However, Bucher and Schneider (1973) have argued that the 'Reinforced Practice training procedure may bias test results favourably in two ways. First, the number of objects in each row was small. Thus, the child might assess or count the objects, and need not watch the transformation. This tactic could then be applied in testing. Some counting ability has been required in most number conservation training studies; and except for Wallach, Wall and Anderson's Doll Addition—Subtraction training all the training conditions . . . permitted the child to see the post-operation object sets. Mermelstein and Meyer (1969) appear to have presented the only training condition in which the number of objects in either set was greater than ten . . . Wohlwill and Lowe's Reinforced Practice . . . used only a conserving operation, so that the reinforced choice after the transformation was always the same: to state that no change had occurred. Again, to learn this, the child need not attend to the transformation. This same artifact was also present within trials: the same response was reinforced both before and after the transformation. Learning this response bias would give good test performance, since in testing only conserving transformations are typically used', pp. 189–190.

Rothenberg and Orost (1969) attempted an approach to the teaching of the conservation of number through the presentation of a logical sequence of component concepts or steps evaluated in a series of three experiments. Training sessions involved reinforced counting (Wohlwill and Lowe, *op. cit.*): addition and subtraction of one object at a time (Gruen, 1965); and verbal training on the concept of 'more' (in number) versus 'longer' (in length). The results of the study implied that conservation of number can be taught to young children; moreover, the effect of training lasted as long as three months and increased the understanding of related problems (details are given in Modgil, 1974, pp. 91–92).

Lally (1968) investigated Braine and Shanks' (1965) hypothesis that verbal stimulation and feedback information accelerate conservation of number and enable children to distinguish between real and phenomenal appearances (details of this study appear in Modgil, 1974, pp. 85—86).

In Beilin's (1965) study, subjects were trained on length and number conservation using non-verbal reinforcement, verbal orientation reinforcement, verbal rule instruction and 'equilibration' methods. The results indicated that 'correct verbalization of the conservation principle, both before and after training, was less predictive of correct performance in conservation tasks than the reverse. On the pre-test, there was little convergence of conservation performance for children who did not fully conserve. Training materially increased convergence, but not to the extent presented among conservers who acquired the capacities less formally.' (*Cf.* Figurelli and Keller, 1972, who report 'the lack of a significant training effect on transfer test performance indicates that training of the type employed did not transfer from one set of conservation tasks to a dissimilar set of conservation tasks. Similar results were reported by Beilin, 1965. It is quite likely that training with this simple procedure results in acquisition that is separate and independent for each conservation concept — and perhaps for each task within a given concept'.)

Winer's (1968) study addressed itself to the effect of 'set' on the acquisition of conservation of number. The general experimental procedure involved addition/subtraction training, perceptual-set training or no-set training together with conflict trials and post-tests. The main investigation comprised two studies: with respect to the first, a significant relationship between performance and training conditions was evidenced, the performance of the addition/subtraction group differed significantly from the performance of the perceptual and control groups. The second study revealed a non-significant difference in favour of the groups receiving the conflict trials (details are given in Modgil, 1974, pp. 86—87).

Field (1974) sought to discover the variables which were critical to the development of Piagetian conservation in ESN children by replicating and comparing the Learning Set method (Gelman, 1969) and the Verbal Rule method (Beilin, *op. cit.*). Three experiments were conducted comprising pre-tests, training sessions and post-tests. Results demonstrated that after the first post-test the Verbal Rule method proved superior to the Learning Set method. The long-lasting results were produced by the Verbal Rule method and the justification answers given by the Verbal Rule — trained Ss in training experiments included the concepts of identity, reversibility, and compensation. (Details follow.)

The training of number conservation in retardates was studied by Lancaster and McManis (1973) where 18 adults were divided into three groups equated for IQ, MA, and number conservation performance. Subjects received either addition—subtraction and reversibility training under either cognitive—conflict or nonconflict conditions, or no training. 'Under cognitive-conflict, transformation of one of two sets of discrete elements produced a perceptual illusion, and the addition-subtraction and reversibility operations applied to that set produced conflict between its length and density. Under nonconflict, simultaneous application of the operations to both sets avoided such conflict. Both training groups made significant gains from pre-test and significantly exceeded controls in post-test number conservation (ps< .05). Lack of differential gains by the training groups suggested that cognitive conflict is not essential to induce number conservation', p. 303. (Details are given later.)

Studies like those of Gruen (*op. cit.*), Smedslund (*op. cit.*) as well as Winer (*op. cit.*) which employed the conflict inducing training technique have been criticized by Kuhn (1974). She argues that, 'Because training trials are not matched to an individual Ss judgments, however, it is not assured that all trials will be of the desired form. For example, an addition may be made to the stimulus the S considers more. Moreover, even when trials are of the desired form, there is no guarantee that the procedure puts the S into conflict; if the E continues to remove elements from the rearranged array that a non-conserving subject claims is longer (i.e., "more"), the S may simply change this response at whatever point in the procedure the array ceases to appear longer to him', p. 597.

A discrimination test was employed by Halford and Fullerton (1970) in order to induce conservation of number. Minor modifications were made to the 'beds and dolls' task and results indicated that the training method induced two-thirds of the subjects to acquire conservation of a 'stable' kind.

Curcio, Robbins and Ela (1971) showed that a combination of readiness and body-part training (i.e. use of fingers) was the most effective for pre-school children in facilitating number conservation with external objects (details of the study are given in Modgil, 1974, pp. 96—97).

Bryant's (1972) study has the implication 'that the emphasis should be shifted to training children how to form judgments properly instead of teaching them invariance'; further, that previous attempts to train invariance have, on the whole, been unsuccessful '. . . because the experimenters were trying to teach children the wrong thing, to teach them, in fact, something which they knew already'. That children as young as three years of age can manipulate the invariance principle has been demonstrated by Bryant. Bryant also indicated 'that training that some cues provide a more reliable basis for quantity judgments than others, enables young children to transfer quantity judgments over perceptual transformations much more effectively than they had previously' (details of the study appear in Modgil, 1974, pp. 99—100, and in Volume Two in the present series *Piagetian Research*).

With respect to number conservation, an interesting extension among the varied training approaches is the study by Feigenbaum (1971) who explored the hypothesis that 'successfully training a child to show conservation will improve his ability to take different social roles and conversely that successfully training a child to take different social perspectives will improve his ability to conserve'. The results indicated a relation between the two aspects of development (details are given in Modgil, 1974, pp. 97—98).

Pertinent here is a reflection by Curcio, Kattef, Levine and Robbins (1972), in relation to some of the above-mentioned studies, *viz.* Beilin, Curcio, Robbins and Ela and Whiteman and Peisach. Curcio *et al.* (1972) argue that '. . . these investigators have relied directly upon the age of the child as an index of susceptibility or differentiation of total non-conservers from partial conservers. Thus, the specific factors responsible for differential susceptibility to conservation training remain open to question because so many conservation-relevant abilities, such as memory, language etc. can covary with these general variables'.

Operational exercises were constructed to train children on the concept of number by Lemerise (1974). A pre-test classified Ss into three groups of pre-operational children. 'In accordance with Piaget's theoretical model on the construction of number, the exercises were based on the generalization of class similarities (group one), the generalization of relational differences (group two), or on both alternately (group three). To measure the effect of the learning exercises, the two number experiments were administered in two successive post-tests (one month interval). It was found that (1) the performance of all three experimental groups was significantly higher than the control group's; (2) the two groups that received only one type of exercise (just class or relation) did not differ from each other; and (3) the group subjected to the two kinds of exercises was significantly better on the second post-test, although the same as the previous two groups on the first post-test'.

Brainerd (1974) maintains that the results of three developmental studies and a training experiment have lent credibility for the ordination → natural number → cardination sequence forecast in the ordinal theory. In his 1973b study, quantification of transitive—asymmetrical relations (ordination) was found to appear earlier in American Ss than quantification of pairs of classes via correspondence of elements (cardination). In his second study, ordination was noted to emerge before natural number and natural number was in turn observed to emerge before cardination. Brainerd and Fraser (1973) replicated the results of the first two studies employing identical ordination and cardination measures. However, Piaget's preferred index of natural number, number conservation, was substituted for addition — subtraction of integers. Brainerd (1973c) in the training experiment, trained five- and six-year-olds on ordination and cardination via comparable procedures. The former proved much easier to train than cardination. Additionally, ordinal training transferred to natural number competence while cardination did not. The inducing of ordinal and cardinal representations of the first five natural numbers was studied by Brainerd (1974). Specifically, he tested the prediction that the ordinal property of natural number symbols was more easily learned than the cardinal property of natural number symbols. Simple feedback procedures were used in pre-schoolers, who evidenced no proficiency with either the ordinal or cardinal properties of natural number symbols, to train them to acquire these properties. Both properties proved to be trainable, with the ordinal property much easier to train than the cardinal property. Moreover, ordinal training effects were more durable across a one-week interval than cardinal training effects. Ordinal training demonstrated transfer better than cardinal training. (Details appear later.)

c. Conservation

Three possible motives may be attributed to the conservation training studies according to Kuhn (1974). She states that 'The most notable is summarized in the adage that to understand a phenomenon we should try to change it. Thus, conservation training studies might shed light on the precise capacities, and perhaps mechanisms, involved in the development of the conservation concept. The least notable is what Piaget has called the American preoccupation with accomplishing things in the least possible time. A third possible motivation is to disprove Piaget's assertion that the attainment of conservation indicates an underlying cognitive reorganization by demonstrating that conservation can be "taught"', p. 590.

To test the hypotheses that questioning on prerequisite skills relevant to conservation will have a positive effect on standard Piagetian tasks, and that controlling situational variables, in particular content and sequence, will reduce measurement errors in tests for conservation, Ayers and Haugen (1973) tested 34 nursery school and kindergarten children within the age range from 59–77 months who were randomly assigned to two experimental groups and a control group. For one experimental group, neutral objects were employed, while for the other, the Ss were questioned about highly attractive objects. Eight items comprising conservation of equivalence were utilized. Post-test results demonstrated that, due to the questioning procedure, conservation was acquired only by Ss over 66 months of age in the two experimental groups. No Ss under 66 months of age in the control group achieved conservation. No significant trend was computed for the attractiveness of test materials.

In Brainerd's (1974) study, 'Separate groups of pre-school children (four- to five-year-olds) were trained to acquire transitivity, conservation, and class inclusion of length via verbal feedback that was contingent on their judgment responses. The principal findings were: feedback induced durable and minimally general improvements in all three skills; transitivity was easier to train than either conservation or class inclusion and conservation was easier to train than class inclusion; there was no evidence that training on any one of the skills tended to transfer to the other two skills; interconcept transfer of training (to weight) was observed for all three skills; interconcept transfer of training was more pronounced for transitivity and class inclusion than for conservation', p. 324. (Details are given later.)

The acquisition and generalization of conservation by pre-schoolers, using operant training was studied by Bucher and Schneider (1973). The authors state, 'Children under five-years-old have rarely shown conservation even after training. In . . . (the) study they were given reinforced training in graduated steps. They first learned to judge numerical equality or inequality of two rows of objects of unequal lengths. Then number conservation was trained in four steps, then conservation of substance and then liquid quantity, in two steps each. Both conserving and non-conserving trials were presented. Over half the children completed all training steps. Their average age was four years, two months. Transfer test trials were included in each step to pre-test performance at the next step. Transfer performance was typically above chance. Mastery of new steps occurred with few errors. Two typical number conservation training procedures that may lead to spurious conserving judgments were investigated: use of conserving trans- formations only, and use of numerically small sets of objects. Both produced inflated test performance. It is concluded that conservation training studies have frequently failed to control for possible artifacts that can produce false positive responding. In examining the present successful training, it is concluded that operant training programmes show considerable potential for developing behaviour skills indicative of conservation, even in pre-operational children. More detailed analysis of the behavioural manifestations of conservation is needed before it can be determined whether such training actually induces conservation as a cognitive ability', p. 187. (Details appear later.)

The five-year-old's conception of the appearance, reality, and identity of physical objects was studied by Langer and Strauss (1972). These concepts were not coextensive in the structure of the young child's cognition. 'Nor are his identity concepts of conservation the cognitive products of his knowledge about appearance and reality. Indeed, his conservation concepts tend to outstrip his judgments about appearance and reality. Moreover, training the child to distinguish more correctly between appearance and reality does not generally affect his conceptions of conservation', Langer and Strauss (*op. cit.*).

To investigate the roles of language, manipulation, and de- monstration in the acquisition, retention, and transfer of conservation tasks including two dimensional space, number, substance, continuous quantity, weight, discontinuous quantity, area, and length, Rattan (1974) employed a stratified sample of 90 grade one conservers. Ss were randomly assigned to four experimental groups and one control group. Non-conservers acquired conservation and retained this acquisition over five week periods. Direct activity and observation learning were equally effective for inducing cognitive changes leading to the criteria. High degree of verbalization was significantly better than low degree of verbalization under both direct activity and observation learning.

Sheppard's (1974) training study examined whether learning of compensation could be employed to induce conservation operativity and lead to generalization. Two experimental and two control groups comprising 80 five- to six-year-old subjects were selected. These children performed at the lower levels of a conservation pre-test. Ss in the experimental groups were administered training sessions, one with water containers, one with plasticine, while Ss in the one control group had experiences with multiplication of relations in a matrix of beakers without water. The Ss in the second control group received no training. 'A significant number of experimental Ss acquired the conservation involved and generalized in post-tests to other conservations, but in almost all instances control Ss did not change. Practice in the anticipation-of-levels type of task leading to compensation in a structural system such as a groupoid for conservation was effective in producing concept acquisition', p. 717. (Details are given later.)

The role of identity, reversibility, verbal rule instruction in conservation was examined by Hamel and Riksen (1973). The study involved 60 children with mean age five years 10 months. 'Each member of two groups of 20 non-conservers was given a different kind of verbal rule instruction that was focused on the conservation of discontinuous and continuous quantity. One of these rule instructions concerned identity and the other reversibility. Twenty Ss who received no training constituted the control group. Both of the training procedures resulted in non-specific transfer to conservation of two-dimensional space, number, substance, and weight. A week later these training effects were still evident. The group which had received the verbal rule instruction focused on identity profited significantly more from the training than did the other group. The explanation offered is that the Ss receiving identity training could incorporate the verbal rule given, since it was compatible with their developmental level', p. 66. (Details follow later.) Hamel (1974) dealt with the Bruner—Piaget debate over whether identity or reversibility was more fundamental to conservation operativity. The author cites the work of Riksen in which the relative effectiveness of identity—based and reversibility—based conservation training treatments was examined. Overall, the evidence on identity—reversibility presented substantiate Bruner's views rather than Piaget's. Hamel also concerned himself with Piaget's obscure structures—of—the—whole concept and generally tended to indicate that the concrete—operational stage is far less unitary than this concept seems to imply.

In a study entitled, 'Control of the conservation response through discrimination learning set training for conserving and nonconserving transformations', Hamilton (1973) established four experimental groups who received verbal pretraining in the terms same and different through a series of oddity problems before beginning training in (a) oddity only (0), (b) no transformation (NT), (c) conserving transformation (CT), and (d) conserving and non-conserving transformation (CT/NCT). Half of the Ss in each group further received a repeat question during training in an attempt to inhibit the likelihood of the S reversing his response when asked twice about the same item. 'Twenty Ss in each group received post-tests on dimensions used in training (mass and number) and not used in training (length and liquid), post-tests to separate logically responding from instrumentally responding Ss, and post-tests to separate reversing from non-reversing Ss'. The results demonstrated 'increasingly effective training for groups receiving NT, CT, and CT/NCT treatments for both specific and nonspecific transfer items. All groups were superior to oddity only (O). Repeated questioning procedures were effective in "inoculating" the children against the tendency to reverse answers in the face of a second, identical question. No differences were statistically significant in the separation of logical from instrumental responses', *ibid.*, p. 1701—A. (Details appear later.)

In Gholson and McConville's (1974) investigation kindergarten children received stimulus differentiation training either with feedback (experimental Ss) or without (controls), prior to a transfer task involving discrimination—learning problems. 'While the error rates among children of both groups were very low during the stimulus differentiation training, during the transfer task the experimental subjects showed better performances than controls on each of seven dependent measures examined. Of particular interest here was the finding that the experimental subjects manifested strategy systems predominately (50 per cent of their problems) while the controls manifested only stereotypes. Thus, it was possible that the stimulus differentiation training with feedback led kindergarten children to manifest strategy systems regardless of their Piagetian stage', Gholson, O'Connor and Stern (1976, p. 64). The latter authors in a study entitled, 'Hypothesis sampling systems among pre-operational and concrete operational kindergarten children', tested 60 pre-operational and 60 concrete operational children. The Ss received stimulus differentiation training either with feedback (experimental groups) or without (control groups), prior to a series of discrimination-learning problems in which a blank-trial probe, employed to detect the child's hypothesis, followed each feedback trial. On seven of eight dependent measures examined, the concrete operational children demonstrated significantly better performances than the pre-operational Ss. Likewise, there were significant differences in favour of the experimental groups on three dependent measures. 'While the results were generally consistent with predictions derived from Piagetian stage theory, it was suggested that this theory must be elaborated to include a perspective derived from conventional developmental learning theory in order to adequately account for these and other data', (*ibid.*, p. 61). (Details follow.)

Two hundred and eighty-six children aged three years six months to eight years five months were administered a pre-test of 37 tasks consisting of seven kinds of conservation (substance, volume, number, weight, length, area one, area two). Out of the initial sample, 129 non-conservers were subjected by Amaiwa (1973) to cognitive conflict through various transformations by 37 exercises, comprising six kinds of conservation, each task repeated twice. The original 37 tasks were then repeated as a post-test. Ninety-six conservers, including some who indicated the ability in the initial test and some who acquired the ability through the training exercises, were subjected to extinction (number, weight, length, and area). These subjects were retested with 15 conservation tasks selected from the initial series. 'The initial test demonstrated that most conservation skills are gained by age eight. The correlation among the tasks was very high. Factor analyses by both principal axis and varimax rotation methods yielded one common factor; area and weight showed slightly different components. Training in conservation yielded positive results. All Ss resisted extinction. It is concluded that "the concept of conservation acquired by training is essentially the same quality as that acquired naturally"', Amaiwa (*op. cit.*).

The effects of training in conservation of tonal and rhythmic patterns on second grade children was studied by Foley (1975). Experimental and control groups were established and the training programme was based on procedures previously found to be effective in improving conservation ability either in music or in other fields of study. The results demonstrated that training facilitated the conservation performance of tonal and rhythmic patterns. Foley recommended that future research should involve longer training periods, training involving conservation in musical areas other than tonal and rhythmic patterns, and training involving grade levels other than the second grade. (Details are given later.)

Two reviews of training studies are those of Brainerd and Allen (1971) dealing with conservation and Kuhn (1974) who furthers the discussion of the issues that Brainerd and Allen's review raised. These latter authors concluded that the evidence substantiates the view that conservation can be induced by short-term experimental means. Their criterion for success of a training study was the statistical significance of the post-test difference between experimental and control groups on what ever index of conservation the experiments used. However, other researchers have insisted on different criteria. Kuhn was intent to evaluate what the training experience consisted of from the subject's point of view, i.e., what was the functional, or effective, stimulus that could be considered responsible for any observed pre-test—post-test change? Likewise, to decide on criteria for evaluating the effects of the training experience. 'The question is, what, precisely, changed from pre-test to post-test, or, put in its popular form, has the subject "really" attained conservation?', (*ibid*., p. 591). In extending these problems, she presented a paper designed to further the discussion of the specific issues raised by Brainerd and Allen with respect to conservation training studies. She discussed the ambiguity of the intent of many of the studies, the lack of agreement on methodological criteria for inferring change, a lack of theoretical agreement as to what a conservation judgement reflects and the difficulty of inducing cognitive restructuring by means of brief interventions. Several suggestions are forwarded for the modification of the training study research strategy. (Details follow later.)

Conservation judgments are learned through three mechanisms: identity (addition − subtraction), compensation and reversibility (Piaget and Inhelder, 1941). Implicit in the Genevan view is the notion that conservation arises as a result of the child's reflecting upon his own activity. Methods of training based upon the three above principles facilitate children's conservation judgments. However, Lifschitz and Langford (1975) have argued that 'The training methods . . . incorporate elements not contained in Inhelder and Piaget's description of the three learning mechanisms. These relate to the manner in which the equality of two quantities is established to the child. Either he is asked to count or measure to establish equality or he is given the judgment of an adult to establish the equality'. Lifschitz and Langford therefore investigated these two aspects of conservation training procedures and concluded that 'counting results in both greater and more lasting learning than an adult judgment. From this and other considerations it is concluded that counting, a mechanism for the cultural transmission of ideas, rather than personal construction, underlies conservation abilities'. (Details are given later.)

The effects of drill on addition—subtraction fact learning; with implication of Piagetian reversibility were examined by Davidson (1975) among 1007 elementary and secondary students. The sample included treatment and control groups from first through the ninth grades. The treatment comprised administering drill on the addition facts. An Addition Facts Test and a Subtraction Facts Test were administered and all Ss were tested three times — at the beginning of the study, after one week and after two weeks. Four scores were considered for each test; 'time', the 'number left out', the 'number missed', and the 'total error'. Results showed that 'On nine scores there were large differences between first and second grade groups . . . results are consistent with what one would expect if first grade students had not formed the concept of addition as an operation with reversibility. The results are consistent with what one would expect if: at the second grade level, addition were conceptualized as an operation with reversibility for a good portion of the students, yet there were a good number for whom this reversibility were limited or inoperative; the concept of addition as an operation continued to develop with a more pronounced reversibility during grades three and four', (*ibid.*, p. 102—A). (Details follow.)

More recently, Murray (1976) asserted, 'A final problem in the conservation literature which might yield to an ecological approach is the question of how the conservations are acquired. While it is beyond the scope of this paper to review the conservation training literature — some several hundred papers in its own right — two points can be made. The first is that the training literature, enduring vigorously as it has for 15 years with every unhappy sign for a continued life, shows a striking discrepancy between the earlier and later studies. The studies of the early 1960s led reviewers like Flavell (1963) and Sigel (1964) to conclude that conservation was unteachable. A decade later Wohlwill (1970) concluded that this negative result "has been largely and effectively superseded by a consistent stream of studies reporting much more positive results regarding the effectiveness of a variety of training procedures". More striking, perhaps, is that many of the later studies, for one reason or another, duplicated the earlier procedures. For example, Gelman's (1969) successful procedure largely duplicates one of Smedlund's unsuccessful ones (1961) . . . The second and concluding point deals with some training studies we have just completed which illustrate how a quest for ecological validity may legitimately turn back on itself and lead profitably to more artificial and removed investigations'. Murray cites the studies of Murray (1972); Silverman and Stone (1972); Silverman and Geiringer (1973); Miller and Brownell (1975); Botvin and Murray (1975); Rosenthal and Zimmerman (1972); and Waghorn and Sullivan (1970). (The majority of these studies have received full treatment in volume five in the present series, *Piagetian Research*). (Murray's 1976 article is described later.)

d. Substance

Smedslund's (1961a) study succeeded in inducing the concept of the conservation of substance by employing the 'cognitive conflict' theory. This provides the greatest promise for success because of its similarity to Piaget's theory of adaptation. Moreover, both adaptation and cognitive conflict processes employ the disequilibrium—equilibrium model . . . This is the system, according to Smedslund, of 'competing cognitive strategies' and he has argued that the creation of such conflict would enhance cognitive reorganization to the extent of inducing the concept of conservation. Smedslund conceives of cognitive conflict as being similar to Festinger's (1957) 'cognitive dissonance'. Smedslund's argument is that, if a child believes that the lengthening of a piece of plasticine makes it heavier (because it is now longer) and yet knows that subtracting a piece from the object makes it lighter, then in those cases where both of these schemata are activated with precisely the same strength, cognitive conflict will occur. However, Smedslund's cognitive theory has not been entirely supported. See, for example, Winer (1968) and Hall and Simpson (1968).

Beilin's (1965) training procedure appears to violate Piagetian theory directly. The 'verbal rule instruction provides the child with a statement of the rule to be applied to the problem in each instance of an unsuccessful trial response on a conservation task'. (p. 326) The study has been discussed earlier.

Bruner's (1964) 'language activation' training involves experimental procedures, which also appear to be inconsistent with Piagetian theory. (Details of Bruner's training procedures may be found in 'The Course of Cognitive Growth', *American Psychologist*, 19, 1964 pp. 2—15.) Bruner's position on training is that adequate linguistic experiences would facilitate the concept of conservation. Activation of language habits would enable the child to be in full mental control of the irrelevant perceptual cues and would encourage the child to employ symbolic processes. ' . . . Improvement in language should aid this type of problem solving'. This differs from Piagetian theory (1967) in that Piaget believes that the mental structure precedes language development.

Sigel, Roeper and Hooper (1966) also succeeded in inducing the concept of conservation of substance by employing a technique which incorporated aspects of the techniques of Smedslund (1961a), Gruen (1965), Bruner (1964) and Wallach and Sprott (1964). The sample was unexpectedly small — 10 children were randomly assigned to two groups of five each. Piagetian tasks of conservation were administered. The authors claimed that the acquisition of conservation of substance followed the acquisition of simpler structures such as multiple labelling, multiple classification, multiple relations and reversibility. More specifically, they maintained that training in these structures, in the order stated, should facilitate the acquisition of conservation. However, an important feature has been pointed out by Lovell (1971) in regard to the Sigel—Hooper study (1966): ' . . . pupils involved had IQs of 130 plus, and they may very well have been at or near the transitional stage anyhow. I think this is a point that one has often overlooked in connection with the Sigel study'. Sigel has modified his position on acquisition of conservation. Rather than suggesting that multiple labelling, classification, seriation and reversibility training, in that order, facilitate conservation, he now suggests that classification and discrimination learning may be among the several variables for conservation. It is interesting to note that Piaget's (1952b) contentions are that for operativity to occur, the child must be able to perform multiple classification, multiple relationality, atomism, reversibility and seriation. It must be pointed out, however, that Sigel's (1966) training originated, at least in part, in the Piagetian theory.

Mermelstein, Carr, Mills and Schwartz (1967) hypothesized that the training procedures, described above, would not be effective in the inducement of the concept of the conservation of substance. However, owing to the greater congruence of Smedslund's (1961a) position with Piagetian theory, they hypothesized that such training would be more successful than the other three training procedures — that of Sigel (1966), Beilin (1965) and Bruner (1964). The authors concluded that none of the four training techniques facilitated the concept of conservation of substance. It was further suggested that language interferes with, rather than facilitates, acquisition of the concept (details are given in Modgil, 1974, pp. 103—104).

Brison (1966) attempted to induce the concept of substance in 24 non-conserving subjects. The control group consisted of 26 children who received no training. Twelve of the experimental subjects demonstrated evidence of conservation operativity. The author concludes 'five of these subjects gave at least four of five correct conservation predictions. The concept transferred to substances (clay, sand) not used in experimental group. The five experimental subjects with four correct predictions performed similarly to subjects possessing conservation before the experiment on an extinction item'.

Five-year-old subjects were questioned to ascertain the degree of acquisition they possessed of the conservation of substance (Mori, 1973). 'Subsequently Ss were presented with facts different from their previous recognition; this aroused conceptual conflict'. It was shown that training given to pre-operational children led to the acquisition of conservation of substance. In the second experiment, the results demonstrated that through training, five-year-olds acquired conservation of weight, volume, and atomism without that of substance; 'the sequence of the acquisition of these concepts is never irreversible, and children who have acquired conservation of substance by the synthetic judgment can perform logical reversible operations in thinking as a result, within the limit of the meaning about the proposition, when they transform the synthetic judgment into the analytic one', Mori (1973).

In five studies with kindergarten children between three years six months and six years four months of age and in three studies with backward children between seven years and 13 years five months of age, Schmalohr and Winkelmann (1969) attempted to induce the concepts of the conservation of quantities and substances by training. Glasses and beads were used as stimuli in the training phase and a substantial number of Ss demonstrated the 'learning' of the conservation of quantities in the task with glasses and beads. However, fewer Ss indicated successful transfer to the conservation of quantities in the task with egg cups and eggs. The transference to the conservation of substance in the plasticine task was relatively very small. Schmalohr and Winkelmann conclude that the success of learning was (relatively) specific to the situation.

Acquisition of conservation through learning a consistent classifactory system for quantities was investigated by Halford (1971). Children performing at the lowest levels of conservation operativity were given learning set training with a view to enhancing operativity by teaching the necessary relationships for it to be inferred. Fourteen out of 16 Ss in the training group acquired conservation in comparison to only four out of 16 in the control group. This was followed by all Ss being given training aimed at convincing them 'that two initially equal quantities may still be substituted for one another in a common measure even if they no longer appear to be equal. Finally all conservers were given a faked demonstration of non-conservation. The Ss who had been trained to conserve did not resist this demonstration, whereas 50 per cent of a group of natural conservers did so', p. 151. The training procedure was discussed in relation to learning and equilibration theory. (Details follow).

e. Weight

Among training studies, the majority have dealt with conservation of number and substance, and relatively few have been concerned with the concept of weight. Smedslund (1961b) carried out several experiments which attempted to teach conservation of weight. The first group comprised 11 children successfully trained in the conservation of weight. They were compared with 13 children who had demonstrated conservation operativity on the pre-test. The extinction manipulation consisted of the surreptitious removal, during the conservation transformation, of a piece of clay from one of two balls, initially equal in weight, followed by a weighing which demonstrated that the weights were now unequal. The subject was required to advance an explanation for the inequality, and he was judged to have extinguished if he did not succeed in giving an acceptable explanation. All 11 trained children extinguished by this criterion; in contrast, six of the 13 natural conservers successfully resisted extinction.

Wallace (1972) draws attention to Piaget's (1959) discussion of Smedslund's attempts to accelerate the development of the conservation of weight and makes the deduction that Piaget would agree with training, provided that the treatment was not regarded as a sufficient feature and that encouragement was given to the establishment of conceptual conflict which would lead to structural reorganization and be conducive to the process of equilibration.

Teaching a verbal rule training is designed to teach the principle that enables the S to make conservation judgments. A S making an incorrect judgment is told the verbal rule of either the type: ' . . . it stays the same even though it looks different. See, I can put them back the way they were, so they haven't really changed', (Beilin, 1965, p. 326) or, 'If we start with an object like this one and we don't put any pieces of plasticine on it or take any pieces away from it, then it still weighs the same even though it looks different', Smith (1968, p. 520). An elaborated version of this method is Gagné's learning hierarchy method

(Kingsley and Hall, 1967). Gagné regards conservation as the end point in a sequence of discriminations, skills, rules, and concepts that the child must progressively master in order to comprehend conservation. Training therefore consists of a graded sequence of tasks or experiences involving measuring, counting, explicit and empirical reinforcement, presentation of verbal rules and demonstrations of reversibility.

Kingsley and Hall, using training based on Gagné's (1962, 1963) learning set procedure, which depended heavily on experience rather than on Piaget's maturational structures, yielded highly significant training effects on weight and length conservation and its subsequent transfer to substance conservation. (Details are given in Modgil, 1974, pp. 106—107.) Caruso and Resnick (1972) lend support to the findings of Kingsley and Hall concerning the power of hierarchical analyses in identifying sequences of learning objectives which can lead to accelerated acquisition of specific cognitive skills.

Smith (1968) reported that Beilin's (1965) methods (*op. cit.*) improved significantly the performance of both non-conservers and transitional conservers, whereas Smedslund's (1961a, *op. cit.*) procedure produced no effect on the conservation performance of either group. (Details are given in Modgil, 1974, pp. 107—108. See also Miller, 1973, who discusses and compares his results to those of Kingsley and Hall, *op. cit.* and Smith, *op. cit.*).

Overbeck and Schwartz (1970) attempted to induce weight conservation through a verbal correction procedure. The investigation had two general problems. 'The first problem is that the training method may have been confounded on two counts. The first confounding was that in one-third of the training tasks, Ss were presented a deformation of one of two equal weight clay balls plus the addition or subtraction of clay from the non-deformed ball. This training may have made functional those mental operations which Piaget has argued are necessary for conservation. Consequently, it could be claimed that mental operation exercise may have been partially responsible for the reported cognitive advance. The second confounding is that this type of training meets the requirements of Smedslund (1961b) as conflict-producing. That is, a potential conflict for an intuitive S exists when he judges a deformed clay object to have less clay and also judges the other to have less because some clay has been removed', Strauss (1974, p. 159). Overbeck and Schwartz assessed Ss' stage usage for only the weight concept. There was no evidence that Ss were not transitional between weight and, for example, length conservation.

An attempt to induce the concept of conservation of weight in ESN children was made by Lister (1969). Results demonstrated that ' . . . it is possible to develop a concept of weight conservation in ESN children using a teaching method, which included active manipulations by the learner and verbal representation with emphasis on identity, subtraction / addition and reversibility' (details are given in Modgil, 1974, p. 108).

Appropriate here is the study by Lister (1972) in which she extends her 1969 and 1970 findings to an investigation concerned with the development of ESN children's understanding of conservation. She concludes 'post-tested after one week and then two months, 30 of the 34 instructed children consistently recognized, generalized and gave reasons for conservation on both post-tests. No control child improved in understanding of conservation by the time of the second post-test' (details are given in Modgil, 1974, pp. 109—110.) Although Lister (1970, 1972) demonstrated that conservation can be taught, 'she used an "eclectic" and unspecified method which varied from subject to subject', Field (1974, p. 237).

f. Liquid

When the child realizes that pouring liquid from one container into another does not change the amount, he has achieved liquid conservation. The child has found that the relation 'shorter than' combined with the relation 'wider than' (by an appropriate amount) produces the resultant of equal quantity, by compensation. Piaget (1952b, p. 13) considers compensation to be a necessary condition for conservation. Cohen (1967) demonstrated that four- and five-year-old children could anticipate the level to which liquid would rise when poured into a container of different width. Piaget and Inhelder (1969) reported that only five per cent of subjects tested conserved without also passing the anticipation-of-levels task. Halford (1970) demonstrated conservation Ss were superior to non-conservation Ss in comprehending equal and unequal quantities in containers of varying dimensions, judging changes in one dimension which compensated for modification in another. Over the age of five years both operational and non-operational Ss demonstrated possession of a partial classificatory system corresponding to conjunctions of height and breadth.

Frank (1966) tested children from the ages of four to seven on the classic test of conservation of liquid quantity. In one condition the materials were in full view, and for several conditions the beakers were screened. In the screening conditions, the S was asked to verbalize what he observed with only the tops of the beakers visible. Under the screening conditions there was an increase in the operational response for each age group. Furthermore, 80 per cent of the five-year-old children and virtually all of the six- to seven-year-olds maintained conservation when the screen was removed. A post-test on an unscreened, transfer task demonstrated a pronounced enhancement in conservation response for the five- to seven-year-old Ss, when compared to pre-test norms. The author maintained that the study demonstrated the potential contribution of verbalization to the acquisition of liquid conservation.

The effects of the three training conditions, initially attempted by Frank, on the acquisition of the concept of conservation were further investigated by Strauss and Langer (1970). The results demonstrated that the screening of misleading cues did not facilitate conservation operativity and no credibility was added to Bruner's 'modes of representation conflict hypothesis'. Furthermore, children at the transitional stage were more likely to conserve and 'change progressively'. (Strauss and Langer's study is described in Modgil, 1974, pp. 114–115.).

A recent study by Siegler and Liebert (1972), investigated the effects of presenting relevant rules and complete feedback on the conservation of liquid quantity task. The authors maintained that 'both rules and feedback facilitated production of correct answers and explanations, with the two treatments operating additively'. Furthermore, results of a one-week follow-up demonstrated that the effects were 'temporarily stable'. However, Overton and Brodzinsky (1972) argue 'it should be noted that while other studies have also demonstrated positive effects for various training conditions — e.g. Frank (1966) showed that a technique for screening misleading cues resulted in better performance on (liquid) conservation tasks — there has been in such studies a general lack of empirical inquiry into whether these effects are general across several years or are limited to the transitional children. This distinction is important because findings of general effect across development suggests that the behaviour involved is in fact learned through the techniques employed, whereas, on the other hand, the limitation of the effect to a specific period suggests that these techniques are activating already present cognitive structures'. Perceptual information in conservation: effects of screening were studied by Miller and Heldmeyer (1975). Variations of the screening method were patterned after Piaget and Inhelder (1971) and Frank (1966), which made it possible to systematically vary the number and type of perceptual cues in the liquid quantity conservation task. Non-operativity among kindergarten Ss increased as the number of cues increased. However, first grade Ss were affected very little by the perceptual conditions. Results suggested that the development of conservation involves several levels, beginning with a concept which can be shown only under facilitating conditions. (Details follow.)

By whatever means the S may learn to ignore the cues, it is the specifically visual display that is claimed to have enticed the S to give a non-operational answer. In perceptual training, the technique is designed to focus the subject's attention away from irrelevant dimensions and toward the relevant dimension of amount. In Gelman's (1969) study Ss were provided corrective feedback when they chose among cues inherent in a conservation problem. Ss with this type of training, started learning immediately and reached an asymptotic learning level of roughly 95 per cent correct responses. Ninety-five per cent and 96 per cent of Ss, on the post-test, in this condition were assessed to be at the concrete operations level for number and length conservation, respectively. The role of attention in Piagetian concepts was therefore investigated by Gelman (1969a). Young non-conservers demonstrated conservation operativity when provided with oddity learning set training. Training was designed to redirect attention from irrelevant dimensions (e.g., length of a row of objects) to relevant dimensions (e.g., number of objects). The author suggested that in the standard procedure used to verify for conservation, children were likely to attend to dimensions that were salient but irrelevant. In particular, when the E alters the appearance of the material during the transformation (e.g., by pouring the liquid into a taller and thinner glass or by spreading out one row of objects), the Ss attention may be drawn to these perceptual changes. Consequently, the child ignores the fact that the amount has not altered. The study demonstrated that children may have some comprehension of quantity but did not demonstrate this understanding when irrelevant perceptual dimensions were very salient. Christie and Smothergill (1970) attempted to partially replicate Gelman's study. They administered her length training procedure to Ss who were pre-tested as not having conserving responses for length tasks. 'This study was different from Gelman's in two . . . ways: (a) No number pre-tests or training were administered, and (b) the children in their study were much younger (3, 6—5, 0). They reported that during training the mean number of correct responses were 61.5 per cent, which is quite a bit lower than in Gelman's study. Even more significant, Christie and Smothergill reported that no Ss conserved on any of the post-test length conservation tasks', Strauss (1974, pp. 163—4). Miller (1973) only partly substantiated Gelman's findings. He examined the role of attention to stimulus dimensions in the conservation of liquid quantity. 'An attention task assessed the relative salience of the height, width, and quantity of liquids. Both kindergarten non-conservers and kindergarten conservers found height most salient. In addition, non-conservers nearly always based their beliefs in non-conservation on height. Conservers (and, to a lesser extent, non-conservers) could also attend to width when there was further questioning. Surprisingly, kindergarten conservers seldom attended to quantity. Third grade conservers found quantity most salient but could easily attend to height and width', p. 129. Miller discussed the results in terms of Gelman's (1969a) study. (Details of the study appear later.)

Gelman reported that learning set training with feedback was superior to 'stimulus change' training in which there was no feedback. However Emrick (1969) who focused on feedback demonstrated that there were few differences between the results of shaping or learning set training on conservation. Friedman and Pasnak (1973) maintain, 'Analyses of the way in which learning sets work indicate that at least four factors contribute to the power these techniques have for inducing concept formation. The "supporting habits" hypothesis is essentially incorporated in Gagné's (1968) theory and holds that success in concept formation depends in part on the acquisition of certain supporting habits which may require more time to be learned than the concept itself. Correct observational, verbal, and comparison responses are among the important supporting habits that must be learned. The efficiency of learning sets in extinguishing "error factors" has been demonstrated empirically and must also be assigned an important role. S's bring many biases and erroneous or irrelevant response tendencies to each problem. Although these error-producing habits drop out as any single example of a concept is learned, they nevertheless return with considerable strength on the first trial of the next example problem. As S learns, he apparently becomes more and more proficient at suppressing these interfering response tendencies ... Another factor that is involved in concept induction through learning sets is stimulus transfer. The important aspects of a stimulus situation ... become progressively differentiated through experience with similar distinctive cues in previous problems. This enables the S to discriminate quickly the relevant aspects of any concrete example of the concept he is acquiring. This type of specific transfer is part and parcel of Gagné's model', p. 334.

Of the linguistic training experiments Inhelder *et al.* (1966) found two effects. Firstly, after training in 'conservation — terms', children giving partial conservation answer on a pre-test were able to express arguments more clearly on a post-test. Secondly, many children stated the two dimensions of the conservation of liquid type but did not achieve conservation. Their general conclusion as to the role of language was: 'First, language training, among other types of training operates to direct the child's interactions with the environment and thus to "focus" on relevant dimensions of task situations. Second, the observed changes in the justifications given for answers suggest that language does aid the storage and retrieval of relevant information. However, our evidence offers little, if any, support for the contention that language learning *per se* contributes to the integration and coordination of "informational units" necessary for the achievement of the conservation concepts. Language learning does not provide, in our opinion, a ready-made "lattice" or lens which organizes the perceptual world. Rather the lattice is constructed in the process of the development of intelligence, i.e., through the actions of the child on the environment and the interiorization of these actions to form operational structures', p. 163.

g. Length

Piaget and others, such as Murray (1965), have shown that the age for the acquisition of conservation of length is between seven and eight. However, Braine (1959) has demonstrated that by using non-verbal techniques it is possible to lower some of Piaget's age norms by more than two years. If Braine's conclusions are valid (see Smedslund, 1963 for a detailed critique), it might be reasonable to hypothesize that the use of essentially non-verbal techniques would allow the child to reveal his acquisition of the conservation of length at an age somewhat younger than seven or eight. Smedslund (1965) has commented on Braine's reply regarding the development of transitivity of length. Braine's position is that 'children normally become capable of making transitive inferences of the types A>B. B>C: ⊃: A>C and A<B. B<C: ⊃: A<C (where '>' means 'longer than' and '<' means 'shorter than') around the age of five years'. Braine's study has been criticized by Bryant (1974) who argued, 'each of his problems involved only three quantities, and therefore the considerable successes obtained by the young children in this experiment could have been achieved without their ever having made an inference at all', p. 43.

Further complications were added to the already conflicting data of Braine and Smedslund by Sawada and Nelson's (1967) study. The authors developed a non-verbal method for training and assessing conservation of length. Their data showed that nearly 100 per cent of the children between the ages of seven years two months and eight years, were conservers of length. Nearly 70 per cent of the children between six years three months and seven years one month were conservers, and about 60 per cent of the children between five years four months and six years two months could conserve. 'It appears safe, therefore, to conclude that the threshold age for the acquisition of conservation of length is between five and six. The hypothesis about the efficacy of non-verbal techniques is therefore accepted'.

Jensen (1969) focuses upon Danset and Dufoyer's (1968) study and makes comparisons of their respective methodologies. Also intent to devise non-verbal methods of assessing transitivity, Danset and Dufoyer centred on bidirectional transitivity. However, Jensen limited his investigation to uni-directional transitivity. His design utilized a training and a test phase. The former was used to establish the relevant dimension upon which the child must attend in order to obtain a lead, the latter consisted of eight trials, in which the elements A, B and C were displayed in a systematic variation. A subject was said to display transitivity when he chose the longest of the three sticks A, on the basis of the information A>B and B>C. When this happened more than five times in the eight test trials, the subject demonstrated transitivity. 'In a group of 20 children, varying in age between 52 and 80 months, half of the group, which was socioeconomically upper-middle class, displayed transitivity of length. However, the youngest child displaying transitivity with six correct test trials was 5½-years-old. The youngest child displaying transitivity with eight correct trials was 6¼-years-old'.

Lindenbaum and Blum (1967), using the standard paradigm of A>B>C, with A>C as the set of terms requiring inference, reported that children demonstrated transitive ability at CA five to six. However, Youniss and Murray (1970) cast doubt on the use of the conventional paradigm. Using additional paradigms they demonstrated that children showed the beginnings of stable transitive ability at CA seven to eight thus confirming the Geneva evidence. Feigenbaum (1974) states, 'The contention among researchers centers on the question of whether or not the test procedure using the standard paradigm eliminates all noninferential clues. With the standard procedure, the child observes the length relationships of three sticks in a three step sequence. First, looking at two sticks − A and B − he observes that A>B. On the second test trial, he observes that B>C. On the third step, the middle stick (B) is removed, but making use of the measurements provided by this middle term, the child can infer the relationship of stick A to stick C (A being greater than C). Researchers questioning this procedure noted that a child might designate stick A as "longer" because he had so named it as "longer" on trial step one. Youniss and Murray (1970, p. 169) stated that "If the child calls A the longer stick on (step) three he might be doing so either because of the measuring data afforded through the middle term or because stick A which was the longer stick before is the more reasonable stick to be called longer again". Hence, in deciding the relationship of sticks A and C the child need not rely on inference; he need merely maintain consistency. Murray and Youniss modified the standard procedure by creating two new paradigms; A>B = C and A = B>C. Using the paradigm A = B>C, if the child is asked to pick, consistently, the longer stick during a three step trial, he can no longer pick A on the basis of having judged it longer on the first trial. In addition, if the child is required to pick, consistently, the "shorter" stick, using the paradigm A>B = C he cannot pick stick C on the third trial because of having named it "shorter" when he first picked it. By adding these paradigms, it was thought all noninferential clues would be eliminated... results indicated that ... "for the younger children, no reliable differences were observed between the control condition and any of the transitivity operations". Of the two age groups (CA five-six to seven and CA eight-four to nine-two), only the older group's results reflected distinct differences; "with the middle term first sequence, subjects made more correct choices in the intermediate and equal middle term paradigms than in the control condition". In addition, they found that the number of correct choices for the different middle term condition was significantly less than for the other two paradigms; in fact, "the different middle term condition did not produce more correct choices than the control condition". With the middle term second sequence, however, no paradigm condition received significantly fewer correct choices than any other; "older Ss made more correct choices on each of the transitivity paradigms compared to control trials"',' pp. 8, 9, 11.

With respect to Youniss and Murray's study, Bryant (1974) argued, '... nothing was done in this study to control for memory failures. No steps were taken either to make the children reasonably familiar with the five quantities first or to check that they remembered the original direct comparison when they were asked the inferential question. Thus the consistent failures which Youniss and Murray found in their younger group could very well have been due to forgetting', pp. 43—44.

Negative effects of the pre-test in training conservation of length was studied by Greitzer and Jeffrey (1973) in 44 children between four and five years two months. 'Two procedures, each consisting of 11 non-reinforced trials, were employed. A fading procedure was developed in which the first trial was a collinear transformation, with subsequent trials successively approximating the standard conservation test', p. 435. The alternative procedure followed Gelman's (1969) learning set training. 'The pre-test may increase the salience of misleading cues, in particular, that of the transformation itself. The absence of this cue in learning set training leads to correct responding, but its reappearance in the post-test produces non-conservation. Pre-tested fading training fails due to the transformation on the collinear trial. Without a pre-test, however, both procedures establish length as the appropriate cue', p. 435. (Details follow.)

In Inhelder and Sinclair's (1969) study all Ss were concrete operational for number conservation but intuitive for length. The aim was to determine if the Ss could become concrete operational for length conservation by having them apply number operations for which they were already concrete operational. It was found that 35 per cent of the Ss made no progress at all, and of the 65 per cent who made progress, 28 per cent became fully operational for length. The remaining Ss presumably became transitional. Strauss and Rimalt (1974) found on the first post-test, around the same percentage of Ss made no progress, but of the remaining Ss who did progress, 88 per cent became fully operational. On the second post-test, 46 per cent made no progress, and 84 per cent of the remaining Ss became fully operational for area conservation. The differences in the comparison of the findings might be, in part, due to the more direct content application of these authors training. 'That is, one of the parameters inherent in area conservation tasks is that the number of equal-sized objects on each area must be equivalent. Despite Inhelder and Sinclair's training procedure, this sort of direct connection between number and length conservation is not as obvious, and this may account for why fewer of their Ss conserved for length', Strauss and Rimalt (*op. cit.*, p. 532). In continuation, the effects of organizational disequilibrium training on structural elaboration were therefore examined by Strauss and Rimalt. The training was based on the organizational disequilibrium model that predicted that the successively alternating application of varied partial structures should lead to cognitive enhancement. Training was more effective within and between concepts for Ss with 'structural mix' than for those who had no measured 'structural mix'. '. . . the number of Ss acquiring an ontogenetically later concept increased as a function of increasing pre-test structural elaboration of ontogenetically earlier concepts; . . . structural application disruption for earlier concepts impeded acquisition of later concepts; and . . . acquisition of later developing concepts influenced structural elaboration of earlier developing concepts', (*ibid.*, p. 526). (Details follow.)

Verbal training and the development of concrete operations in adult mental retardates was examined by Svendsen (1973). Following a pre-test two groups of adults were matched with respect to CA, MA, and level of performance on four Piagetian tasks. Each group comprised 18 Ss with the average CA of the experimental group being 36 years and the average CA of the control group was 35 years eight months. MAs of the experimental and control groups on the Columbia Mental Maturity Scale was five years five months and five years four months respectively. Ten training sessions were administered to each S in the experimental group. Each training task comprised measuring two pairs of sticks followed by drawing a transitive inference about the two measured sticks. Five subtests of the Wechsler Preschool and Primary Scale of Intelligence were given to the control group. Post-tests were administered after the training sessions. 'In the experimental group a significant improvement was found on the transitivity test of length

($p<0.001$). This effect had not disappeared on a post-test three months later and on another post-test two years after the training ($p<0.01$, $p<0.02$). The Ss showed an improvement in both making transitive inferences and verbal explanations about the inferences. At the first post-test the improvement on the other tasks based on Piagetian theory was not significant. The Ss in the control group did not improve their performance on tasks based on Piaget's theory . . . this group made a significant improvement on the Columbia Mental Maturity Scale ($p<0.025$). This effect, however, had disappeared two years later', (*ibid.*, pp. 3—4). (Details follow.)

h. Space

Piaget and Inhelder (1956) regarded the concept of horizontality as part of a larger structure, a cognitive Euclidean coordinate system of frames of reference which incorporated horizontality with verticality. By requiring children to fill in the water levels on drawings of bottles set at different angles, Piaget and Inhelder found developmental stages for the child's understanding of horizontality. Children's conceptions of horizontality were resistant to change, as they persisted in erroneous answers that were typical of their particular level of development. Smedslund (1963) substantiated this finding. He noted that Ss who completed a pre-test of drawing water levels and then were shown a real bottle of water filled at various angles did not benefit from this period of observation in a subsequent post-test. Smedslund's view of the Piaget and Inhelder position was, 'The subject can only observe horizontality and deviations from it if he already has a schema of horizontality, and in the absence of this schema, no amount of observation will influence him', (*ibid.*, p. 195). Smedslund considered that feedback was not instrumental in bringing about changes in the child's representation of horizontality. However, Sheppard (1974a) has argued that, '. . . in his experiment the feedback provided was very limited. The Ss in the present experiment generally showed no better performance when observed by E during training than did Smedslund's Ss, when given a view of the various angles of the bottle on only one occasion', p. 197.

However, Beilin *et al.* (1966) in their training study showed an enhancement of the horizontality concept. The most successful procedure involved perceptual confirmation. A demonstration of water was presented covered with an opaque stocking, and was placed in one of eight positions, varying by 45 degrees. For each position S predicted the water level and then compared his prediction with the actual level. After 16 training trials, horizontality test performance (scored out of eight) increased by about two points of score. More recently, Sheppard supported Beilin *et al.* that the most successful technique used in their study was a perceptual confirmation method. Sheppard argued that 'the training study by Beilin *et al.* (1966) was successful because children on the pretest gained mean scores of about four-and-a-half to five out of eight, and were already advanced in concept development and construction of an appropriate schema. However, such an intepretation would be more difficult if Ss were used who on pre-test only succeeded in drawing the water line correctly for a bottle standing in its normal position. Further, it would be difficult to apply to Ss who also were correct when the bottle was completely inverted by rotating 180 degrees, but failed on all other positions of the bottle', pp. 191—192.

The tests of a mathematical group in Sheppard's study were administered because they involved rotations, and because the training procedure required that the Ss who had difficulty had to rotate the materials to find a solution. The data indicated that there was a relation between the two activities — of handling the rotations in the mathematical group and of acquiring horizontality through training. 'In an earlier study on mathematical groups (Sheppard, 1974) a different test of groups was used, involving many more tasks and requiring a learning sequence. However, the ability to make combinations of rotations, and to map them, was found to come with the development of concrete operations, as tested in the areas of conservation . . . That finding has been extended, then, in the present study, to incorporate the relation between ability to map in a mathematical group and ability to benefit from a horizontality training procedure', Sheppard (1974a, p. 197—198). A pre-test—post-test design training was conducted, using a sample of 215 children in grades two and three as a basic sample. From these, Sheppard selected 60 Ss who were non-operational on a test of the concept of horizontality, and randomly allocated to a training experimental group, training control group, and no-training control group. Ss in the experimental group improved significantly after training, the controls did not. Horizontality post-test scores of the experimental group computed .5 and .6 with their scores on a previously administered test of mathematical groups (Sheppard, 1974). Some Ss who showed enhancement after training confused the horizontal with the vertical. Sheppard interpreted such confusion as an indication that the subject was approaching operativity. (Details are given later.)

While investigating the induction of linear-order concepts, Pufall (1973) made a comparison of three training techniques. Forty-five children 'who had failed to attain criterion on three tests of linear order were trained under one of three conditions. Reciprocity training gave the child practice in constructing orders identical with (ABC) or the reciprocal of (CBA) a model (ABC). Reversibility training included reciprocity training and experience predicting and observing the outcome of a 135 degrees rotation and its reverse (−135 degrees). Discrimination training required the child to identify pairs of orders as identical, reciprocals, or different (e.g., ABC to ACB). Under all three conditions children demonstrated learning during training and significant specific transfer effects, while only reversibility training led to generalized transfer to all three tasks during post-testing', p. 642. (Details appear later.)

The investigation by Cox (1976) although primarily concerned with the developmental changes which occur as the child learns to represent another person's view (perspective ability), the author employed a training programme in order to produce conditions conducive to the study of the causes of transition from stage to stage (experiment 6). Three feedback methods of training were compared in experiment 7. Although children who moved to the other observer's position to check their responses improved their performance compared with controls, they did not sustain this superiority or transfer their learning to other tasks; training which provided feedback (visual or verbal) about another's view while the child was confronted by his own view proved more successful. (Details follow.)

i. Time and Speed

Piaget (1969) applied the idea of groupings to the development of the child's concepts of motion, velocity and time, therefore, pertinent here is a developmental study of Piaget's groupement model of the emergence of time and speed concepts undertaken by Weinreb and Brainerd (1975). 'Three key predictions of Piaget's groupement model of middle-childhood cognition were examined . . . (a) The respective composition and reverse operations of two of the eight structures posited in the groupement model (Groupement I and Groupement V) should emerge synchronously in each of the two concept areas. (b) The two structures themselves should emerge synchronously in each of the two concept areas. (c) Between the two concept areas, the two structures should both emerge in the speed area before either emerges in the time area. The findings failed to support either prediction "a" or prediction "b", and they were only partially consistent with prediction "c". However, the findings concerning predictions "a" and "b" were consistent with other recent developmental evidence on the emergence of groupement structures in concept areas other than speed and time', p. 176. (Details follow.)

The development and training of time concepts in young children was examined by Ziegenfuss (1973). A time concepts test was developed with three parts: seriation, duration, and coordination. One hundred girls, between the ages of three years 10 months and eight years seven months from lower and middle class backgrounds constituted the sample. Both age and social class differences were statistically significant on the total score and the three subtests. These scores substantiated the developmental aspect of time concepts since there was a consistent increase in scores from pre-kindergarten to second grade. Social class was a significant variable for both total and subtest scores, with the middle class girls performing at the higher levels. A training programme was implemented for 46 girls and 59 boys designed to teach simpler ideas involved in time concepts. The Ss in the control group received no training and continued their normal activities. Half of the Ss in both the experimental and control groups were pre-tested. All of the Ss were post-tested to determine the effects of training, social class, sex, teacher, pre-test, and order of presentation of the testing items. The study indicated that training was effective on a selected aspect of cognitive development—time concepts. Moreover, that such training could be undertaken by regular classroom teachers with groups of children in a regular kindergarten programme. (Details are given later.)

The development and inducement of time concepts through conflict based on a primitive duration capacity was studied by Berndt and Wood (1974). Ss, aged five and seven years, compared the relative time for which two trains travelled. 'Children made accurate duration judgments when using only auditory cues (whistles), indicating that a primitive capacity for judging duration exists. When visual and auditory cues were available, children tended to use a distance model, that is longer distance = longer time. The children experienced conflict when an initial choice based on auditory cues was shown to be incompatible with the distance model. Various attempts to resolve this conflict were compared. Some solutions seemed to indicate development toward operational time concepts. The results were contrasted with Piaget's (1969) theory of the development of time concepts, and the usefulness of the method in diagnosis of cognitive development was discussed', p. 825. (Details follow.)

The effects of instruction in the concept of speed and proportions on children in the third grade were investigated by Boulanger (1974). Fifty-one Ss who could perform simple division and who were concrete operational in their conception of space, time and speed were randomly assigned to two instructional treatment groups and a control group. 'The training and comparison treatment was a sequence of problems, questions, and demonstrations interwoven with training in the concept of speed and simple proportions. The comparison only treatment was the same sequence of problems, questions, and demonstrations but without training in the concept of speed and simple proportions. All instruction in both treatments was done on an individual basis. The control group received no instruction dealing with speed and proportions. Three dependent measures were administered on an immediate and on a delayed basis. Immediately after the completion of instruction, children in the treatment groups were individually administered measures of retention, transfer, and transfer to two Piagetian tasks. Three weeks later, three similar measures were administered again individually. The control group children were individually administered the same measures at about immediately the same times as the treatment group children'. Boulanger concluded that concrete operational children could be trained to successfully perform on an immediate basis a speed comparison task. However, such a training demonstrated neither durability nor generalization to other tasks of proportion. (Details follow.)

Cognitive style and reasoning about speed was investigated by Ehri and Muzio (1974). A test for field dependency was administered to college students with the question to reason about the relative speeds of horses turning on a merry-go-round platform. 'To promote the recognition that horses located on the outside of the platform travelled faster than horses on the inside, additional problems were presented which directed subjects' attention to the relevant variables'. Unlike field independent Ss who reasoned correctly from the outset, field dependent Ss failed to think analytically. Perceptually salient features of the situation together with centration contributed to their lower performances. (Details appear later.)

j. Logic

Conflicting evidence has emerged with respect to the role of training in logical thinking. Ss in Simcox's (1970) study were administered games built on logic. Her results demonstrated that a structural training in logic tended to enhance such performance. Likewise, Burt (1971) in a review of the related studies maintains that logical thinking in children can be enhanced. Peel (1968) also, is among those who advocate the deliberate teaching of logical thinking. However, Ennis *et al.* (1969) demonstrated that training seven- to nine-year-olds in 'conditional logic' resulted in no differences between the experimental groups and the control. Pre-operational children in a complex problem-solving skill when subjected to training demonstrated that while some skills may be induced, problems involving combinatorial skills proved abortive (Anderson, 1965). Beilin (1971) attributes the conflicting results to the ill-defined criteria employed for judging operativity. He asserts that the lack of agreement among psychologists as to the nature of operativity leads to disagreement in the interpretation of data. Bryant (1971) infers that training in logical abilities in young children is not necessary, instead efforts should be directed to such factors as memory capacity which impede the effectiveness of these logical abilities.

i Class inclusion

Kohnstamm's studies in 1962 and 1966 (Kohnstamm, 1967) demonstrated the facilitative value of the training programmes involving verbal explanation, in class-inclusion tasks. Although several other researchers have attempted to bring forth the inclusion response (Ahr and Youniss, 1970; Wohlwill, 1968), these have not succeeded in establishing conclusively that young children five to six years of age can acquire the ability to comprehend inclusive relation of classes. Hatano and Kuhara (1972) have criticized Kohnstamm's studies (*op. cit.*). 'The first is that he explained to children, and then asked them to explain the inclusion response in terms of number of two given classes . . .

numbers obtained by counting do not imply any logical relation between two classes . . . Though he used varieties of transfer items, most of them could be solved by mere generalization of the response and this left a possibility of interpreting the findings as mere response learning.' Hatano and Kuhara utilized an extensive training programme on class-inclusion problems, among 13 five- to six-year-old subjects. The authors' 'most important conclusion is that children of five to six years of age can acquire the ability to grasp inclusive relation, as typical of logical relations of two classes. Using more adequate methodology than Kohnstamm's, we confirmed this assertion that an intensive training programme is effective' (see also Okonji's study on the effect of special training on the classificatory behaviour of some Nigerian Ibo children, 1970, described in Modgil, 1974, pp. 240—241).

Aldrich (1970) reported that a combination of verbal and manipulatory training produced significant gains in classification inclusion skills. The results were interpreted as representing an 'isolated schema' rather than a general conceptual ability. Sigel, Roeper, and Hooper (1966) employing a training procedure found that training programmes focused on classification influenced subsequent cognitive structures. This type of classification training produced generalized conceptual enhancement. Olmstead, Parks, and Rickel (1970) demonstrated gains in children's ability to group items following training. In a follow-up assessment a year later, the training was found to have had a durable effect.

Conservation of part and whole in the acquisition of class-inclusion was examined by Sheppard (1973). An identity transformation and a transformation of addition were incorporated in a training programme for class-inclusion. The study drew from a sample of 104 Ss aged six years, an experimental and a control group of 21 Ss each. The test of class-inclusion, comprising 10 items, was administered in a pre-test— post-test design to assess concept changes brought about by training. An overall enhancement was noted in the experimental group only. 'Support for the operation of internal factors in cognitive development was provided by an obtained increase from first to second post-test scores. Two conservations were considered to be involved — conservation of the whole and of the part', p. 380.

Training comparison of the subset and the whole set: effects on inferences from negative instances were studied by Knight and Scholnick (1973). 'Five-year-olds inferred the relevant cue from four possibilities (boat, ball, bear, and doll) after being informed whether the cue was present in each of two stimulus pairs like bear—ball, boat—ball. Sixty-four children failing to identify the cue from two negative instances were assigned to one of four training procedures: comparison of instances with the entire stimulus set, comparison of similarities and differences between instances, combination of these two, or stimulus exposure. Groups trained to compare the whole and subset improved in cue identification from negative instances; performance in the stimulus exposure group declined. The combined training group also improved their inferences about two positive instances', p. 162.

ii. Simple classification skills

A study of the role of manipulatory grouping experience in the classification skill development of young children was undertaken by Koon (1974). 'A training programme was implemented with 36 four-, five-, and six-year-old middle class Caucasians from middle to upper socioeconomic families, who were randomly assigned to three experimental conditions having 12 Ss each, two training groups and a control group. The training consisted of a series of 20 individually conducted, developmentally sequenced, manipulatory grouping experiences with objects through the use of sorting formats, both with and without teacher—child interaction'. The tests were adapted from the Kofsky Scalogram of Classificatory Behaviour (1966) used in pre- and post-testing procedures, and The Object Categorization Test, active conditions (Sigel, Anderson and Shapiro, 1966), used in a post-test only. Koon concluded that the manipulatory grouping experience is successful in positively modifying the classification skill competence of young middle class Caucasian children, only in combination with teacher—child interaction. However, both types of training were successful in enhancing greater flexibility of grouping behaviour. (Details follow.)

Klein (1974) attempted to induce classification skills in trainable mentally retarded children. The sample comprised 41 children within the IQ range 30 to 50 and aged six through 12 years. Ss were randomly assigned to experimental and control groups. A six week intervention was devised for the treatment group to induce classification skills. The training focused on 'manipulation and exploration of meaningful, concrete materials, leading to the subjects' comprehension of these items in terms of their dimensional attributes of form, size and colour. As soon as these concepts were grasped, Ss were helped to construct groups of like objects of a selected attribute. The intervention included training in classification on single, double and triple schemes, using meaningful familiar toys. Test materials included concrete meaningful objects in the Toy Classification Task. (TCT) and abstract blocks in the Object Sorting Task (OST), to compare Ss responses to concrete and abstract materials. The tests administered immediately following the invervention, were referred to as short term acquisition test (STAT) those administered seven weeks later were referred to as long term retention test (LTRT).' Results of tests with the TCT on all schemes demonstrated that the experimental group showed significant better performance than the control group at the p<.01 level. No significant differences among sorting preferences were noted. Likewise, no significant differences were computed between the performance of the experimental and control group on the OST. 'Long term retention test results indicated that the experimental group did maintain its advantage over the control group with the meaningful concrete items in the TCT on single, double and triple classification tests. On the OST for LTRT the experimental Ss performed significantly better than controls. There was a high correlation, .70, p<.01, between the sorting scores of the experimental group on concrete and abstract materials in STAT. This high correlation was not maintained in LTRT', (Klein, *op. cit.*, p. 4479A). (Details follow.)

The effects of instruction on length relations on the classification, seriation, and transitivity performances of 81 first and second grade children were examined by Johnson (1974). The Ss were divided into experimental and control groups. The former group of children were given experiences in sorting and seriating linear objects. On the seriation test, the main effects of treatment and grade were significant. 'Grade and school effects were significant on a conservation test, with only school effect significant on a transitivity test. No significant relationship could be detected between classification and transitive ability using "same length as", or between seriation and transitive ability using "shorter than" and "longer than" '.

Using Bruner's (1966) tests of equivalence (verbal and non-verbal) as the criteria, training in logical thinking and its effects on the grouping strategies of eight-year-old children was investigated by Burke (1974). Overall the training enhanced the performance in favour of the boys but not for the girls, the training x sex interaction being significant for performance in the verbal test. 'Again, for both tests, more of the experimental group displayed above-average groupings in the functional and nominal categories, the difference from the controls being statistically significant', p. 311. (Details appear later.)

iii. Multiple classification skills

Sigel, Roeper and Hooper (1966, discussed earlier) agree on the feasibility of training children to conserve, and they indicate the need for two other experiences; multiple classification and multiple relationship. These operations are prerequisites for logical reasoning. Sigel and Shantz (cited in Shantz and Sigel, 1967) compared the performance of Ss given multiple labeling—classification and discrimination—memory instruction to that of a control group (average age four years 10 months) on quantity, weight, and area conservation tasks.

Significant gains on quantity and weight conservation were observed. Children who showed lower levels of conservation performance but were operational on a pre-test of relational term comprehension (Griffiths, Shantz, and Sigel, 1967) were assigned to a training condition (four labeling–classification and two discrimination–memory groups). Little difference between the two instructional conditions with respect to classification, seriation, reversibility, or conservation task performances were recorded after post-testing. Hooper (1972) studied classification and seriation training conditions in children aged three years six months to four years six months in small group instructional settings. Classification instruction was not effective, whereas seriation instruction demonstrated significant specific transfer. Further, this transfer was mostly present for the older Ss. No far transfer to conservation task performances was noted. Caruso and Resnick (1972) have reported similar task analysis approaches to be effective in facilitating children's dual classification skills. Task structure and transfer in children's learning of double classification skills was examined by Caruso and Resnick. '. . . experiment tested a task analysis and hypothesized hierarchy of double classification tasks. Twenty-six kindergarten children were trained on three different matrix tasks in either the optimal (simplest to most complex) or reverse sequence. More optimal sequence Ss learned the tasks, and they learned in fewer trials than did reverse sequence Ss. These results, together with the pass-fail patterns among the tasks, confirm the hypothesized relationship. They also suggest the power of hierarchically sequenced training in the acquisition of specific cognitive skills. Positive transfer to an untrained matrix task with similar task structure lends further support to the task analysis on which the hierarchical predictions were based', p. 1297. (Details are given later.)

In continuation, the efficacy of small group instructional programmes in classificatory, seriation, and combined class/series skills was examined by Bingham-Newman and Hooper (1974) in 60 urban, middle class four- to five-year-old Ss in a transfer of training design. For the seriation instructional condition significant specific transfer effects were observed. However, little differences were noted for the classification, verbal intelligence, and far transfer conservation task measures. No evidence was found for the sex differences, school location effects, teacher biases, and pre-testing effects. 'The apparent feasibility of seriation skill instruction for preschool aged children and the general non-effectiveness of the classification and combined instructional conditions, particularly insofar as far transfer effects are concerned suggests a non-unitary picture of cognitive functioning during the transitionary phases between pre-operational and concrete operations period thought', (*ibid.*, p. 379). Bingham-Newman and

Hooper further maintain that 'the failure of the present classification training to influence the children's performances on the complex class addition and inclusion tasks significantly is perhaps understandable in view of the typical age norms associated with these tasks (*cf.*, Brainerd and Kaszor, 1974; Klahr and Wallace, 1972). The higher level tasks assessing class additivity relationships are clearly linked to the developmental status of the target children and generally have not been readily modifiable via instructional programming (*cf.*, Beilin, 1971; Klausmeier and Hooper, 1974)', p. 390. (Details appear later.)

A series of studies, directly or indirectly related to the teaching of the completion of a matrix utilizing two attributes, were undertaken by Jacobs and Vandeventer (1968, 1969, 1971, 1971a). Their 1968 study indicated that an overall enhancement in the manipulation of double-classification problems could be achieved by altering certain features in the training phases. In continuation, Jacobs and Vandeventer (1971) established a number of training sequences, each of which permitted more individualization of instructions and involved more verbalization. A new test of double-classification skill was substituted for Coloured Progressive Matrices. Children in the experimental group (with highly structured and individualized training) performed at a higher level of classificatory operativity involving colour and shape relations than children in the control group. This acquired ability in the experimental subjects was also transferable to related post-tests involving new stimuli, both immediately and four months later. (The study is described in Modgil, 1974, pp. 120–122). Jacobs and Vandeventer (1969) carried out a survey of the actual rules employed in current double-classification test items. They were able to establish a 'universe', within which transfer could more meaningfully be assessed. The authors in their 1971a study, defined a 'universe,' 'as consisting of all possible pairings of twelve logical relations . . . '. They wanted to assess transfer from the training procedure of their 1971 study within this 'universe'. An evaluation of the effects of more extensive training together with the effectiveness of different trainers was made. The results indicated that '"regular-training" subjects significantly outperformed control subjects throughout the universe of relations. "Extended training" produced significantly more transfer than "regular training". The two trainers did not differ in effectiveness. Transfer effects for regular and extended training were found to hold up three months later'.

Parker, Rieff and Sperr (1971) examined the effectiveness of a hierarchical instructional programme in multiple-classification. Overall, the evidence indicated an enhancement in the ability of the six- and seven-year-olds from the training programme. However, the four-and-a-half-year-old children demonstrated little increase in multiple-classification ability. The authors, in explaining the latter finding, advance two possible explanations: first, that the four-and-a-half-year-old children were too young to profit from multiple-classification instruction, and second, that the training programme needed revision (details appear in Modgil, 1974, pp. 124–126).

In continuation, Parker, Sperr and Rieff (1972) employed two multiple-classification training programmes: an individual sequenced instruction (patterned after Gagné, 1965, 1966; Resnick, 1967) and terminal objective instruction (patterned after Jacobs and Vandeventer, 1968, 1969). Seventy-two children who were non-operational on multiple-classification problems, each at ages five years six months, six years six months and seven years six months were involved in the study. Overall, the results demonstrated that 'both individual sequenced instruction and terminal objective instruction groups performed significantly better after training than the contact control group, but that the individual sequenced instruction and the terminal objective instruction groups did not differ from each other on total score, criterion performance, or transfer tasks'. Moreover, the children aged six years six months and seven years six months benefited more from the training programme than the five-and-a-half-year-old subjects. (Details appear in Modgil, 1974, pp. 124–5.)

To investigate whether training in attention and classification enhanced children's performance on Piagetian tests, Sigel and Olmsted (1970) tested Negro children enrolled in a Head Start programme. A four-week training on certain skills and concepts was administered. A year after training, these children were compared with a matched control group on five Piagetian tests of number, quantity, multiple classification, multiple seriation, and reversibility. No significant effect on performance in any of these tests was computed. 'These results cannot be attributed to a lack of understanding of concepts like more, same, or less, since tests for this were administered. All children passed this test . . . It is important to point out that the difficulties these first grade children have (both at the beginning and at the end of first grade) in not being able to conserve number and / or mass, reveals the seriousness of their cognitive deficit, especially of the criterion used in our data from middle class whites. It is worth pointing out that among five-year-old white middle class children, conservation of number and mass are soluble. Of the 75 (white) children tested . . . approximately 50 per cent could conserve in these areas without training and after a nine-session training programme, 68 per cent of the previous non-conservers could then conserve', Sigel and Olmsted (*op. cit.*, p. 328). Of the Negro Head Start Ss who received four weeks training, 81.3 per cent were non-operational on number and 93.2 per cent non-operational on quantity either before or after training.

Ellis (1972) postulated that the cognitive strategy which effectuates conservation is the result of the fusion of a number of crucial mental operations and that the sequential acquisition of these prerequisites would construct the cognitive structure necessary for conservation to be discovered as a principle. The sample of 105 children was divided into three age groups, with age ranges of six years four months to seven years one month, five years six months to six years three months, and five years to five years five months. Ss were randomly assigned to one of three treatment groups − 'structured', 'free' or 'control'. Eight training sessions were designed to offer children experiences of classification and multiple classification, relationality and multiplicative relationality. Operations of atomism were incorporated via which the cognition of the reciprocity of the dimensions of equal masses might be acquired. A ninth session of the 30 minutes duration, as were the others, offered training in reversibility with the aim of consolidating the crystalising cognitive structure. 'It was found that conservation can be discovered as a principle via a logical sequence of experiences designed to develop a strategy for the handling of perceptual cues. Conservation was acquired when the exact reciprocity of relationships after deformation was understood and the carrier of this information was atomism. The strategy, once learned, generalized in varying degrees across the horizontal *décalage*. Other factors might well impede its application in some conservation situations. Conflict / equilibration methods of training were effective and produced durable learning which resisted extinction'. 'Free' methods, as defined, were less effective than the 'structured' training. Backward children were able to build the cognitive structure of conservation and to use the then available strategy. Future training attempts based on conceptual analysis may well lead to effective teaching methods. (Details are given later.)

The hypothesis of a multimedia feedback system, as elaborated by Steiner (1974) has received support from Kohnstamm (1963, 1967), Ojemann and Pritchett (1963), and Seiler (1968) studies, where the experimenter himself gives feedback in a verbal or nonverbal manner. It is this kind of learning experiment that leads to high operational success. Such experiments clarify what Aebli (1970) has pointed to: the child does not acquire operational structures necessarily through cognitive conflicts and the corresponding equilibration processes; there is construction without conflict and without equilibration processes in Piaget's sense, for example, in the case that an adult is teaching or explaining a certain fact to a child.

One of the most efficient training techniques seems to be the mobility training (Montada, 1968) where the point of departure is a modification of Piaget's concept of mobility. Behavioural mobility may be considered as the ability to realize numerous actions in quick succession, all relating to the same object or situation, and to integrate them into a systematic whole (Piaget's *structures d'ensemble*). Montada begins with states of low mobility, (at the pre-operational level). 'His training procedure consists in mobilizing some or all possible actions referring to the same object. The child thus brings together single actions, constitutes relations among them, and finally integrates them into a system. This procedure is intended to mobilize what Piaget calls the *mise en relation* (putting into relationship). Montada's Ss show operational success in logical multiplication (matrices) and in inclusion problems. Even if the essential construction processes take place at a microlevel, in a manner as yet insufficiently known and controlled, Piaget's concept of *mise en relation* — dynamically interpreted as the basis for the mobility procedure proves to be extremely productive', Steiner (1974, p. 897). Steiner extended the mobilizing idea to the logical multiplication of asymmetrical transitive relations (multiple ordering). The sample comprised 67 children within the age range from six years six months to eight years one month. The Ss were presented with a matrix with round wooden blocks of four different colours and four different sizes in an ordered way. 'The aim was to teach the child, after removing the blocks from the matrix board and mixing them up, (1) to reconstruct the matrix . . . and (2) to transform it, starting from one given block put at a certain place by the E . . . After a pre-test, all children received special mobility training for mobility (1) of classification, (2) of seriation, and (3) of direction. In the typical mobilizing procedure, the child had to carry out several actions on the same selected set of three, four, or five blocks, but always had to change the actual cofiguration', p. 897. Ikonically trained children were superior to the symbolically trained Ss. 'Such an assumption has to be viewed critically, however . . . To continue the exploration of the construction process, especially concerning verbal representations at a microlevel, I recently used blocks of more complex forms and an easy symbolic form of number cards. The outline of the experiment remained the same. The hypothesis related to the fact that construction processes of cognitive structures do not so much depend on the media of representation at a macrolevel but rather on the extent and the kind of the representations in microprocesses. In fact, the symbolically trained children of these recent experiments were superior to their ikonically trained peers; the latter, moreover, consumed much more training time,' pp. 898—899.

More recently, Carlson and Dillon (1976) maintain, 'An important aspect of the activation model (Overton, 1975) which should be stressed is that totally new structures are not formed or acquired for the first time during the testing period (*cf.* Aebli, 1961; Seiler, 1968), they are simply brought to use. The preponderance of evidence from various training studies on conservation supports this, as typically only children at transitional stages seem to be affected by the experimental manipulations (Beilin, 1971; Inhelder, Sinclair and Bovet, 1974). Thus, it might be concluded that activation is involved in training effects'.

Matrices and Order of Appearance tests were administered to 46 second grade children who were randomly divided into two groups, Carlson and Dillon (1976). One group was given the tests in the standardized manner, the other in a nonstandardized way in which feedback was given and discussion allowed. Each child was tested individually and given the test on two occasions, the second being standard conditions for all Ss. Standardized math and reading achievement scores were obtained as well as teachers' judgments of math and reading achievement and potential. Significant differences due to condition and time of testing were found for both the Matrices and Order of Appearance tests. The correlations with scores on these tests given in the nonstandard condition and second testing tended to be highest with teacher judgments of achievement and potential but the magnitude of this interaction was found to be nonsignificant. The results were discussed in terms of performance and competence. It was suggested that activation processes may need be involved to avoid Type II error in cognitive tests such as these. (Details follow.)

iv. Formal operational reasoning

Brainerd (1970) and Brainerd and Allen (1971) suggested that the conservation problems may be categorized into those which are solved during the 'concrete' operations and those of 'formal' operations. An attempt to train the formal operational concept of density conservation was made by Brainerd and Allen (1971a) while investigating the effects of feedback and consecutive similar stimuli. A highly significant training effect was evidenced for the feedback treatment. 'The nontrivial nature of the training concept was demonstrated via significant ($p < .005$) pre- to post-test improvements in the feedback subjects' rationales for their answers (intraconcept generality) and via significant ($p < .005$) transfer of density training to solid volume conservation (interconcept generality)'. Details of this study are given in Modgil, 1974, pp. 119−120. (See also Tomlinson-Keasey, 1971, who demonstrated that the training procedure utilized, produced an overall enhancement in tasks of formal operations, in adult females aged 11 to 54 years. However, such an acquired ability was not transferable to related, but delayed post-tests). (The details are given in Modgil, 1974, Chapter Five). However, Kuhn and Angelev (1975) found support 'for the existence of the cognitive stage of formal operations, and the . . . study provides counter evidence for recent claims that "training" studies cannot provide such evidence or that developmental stages are empirically unverifiable (Brainerd, 1973, 1974)'. (The Kuhn and Angelev study appears in Volume 3 in the series *Piagetian Research*, pp. 233–34).

In an attempt to induce formal operational reasoning performances, Berzonsky, Lombardo and Ondrako (1975) randomly assigned 67 introductory psychology students to experimental and control groups. The logic tests were constructed from items used by Roberge (1971, p. 339). The experimental condition involved solving logical syllogisms when the obvious 'logical error' was not included as a possible answer. Subjects in the control group solved the identical problems with the 'logical error' included as a choice. The pre-test–post-test enhancement demonstrated that the experimental group Ss did significantly better than the control group Ss on invalid principles. Berzonsky, Lombardo and Ondrako discussed the results within the Piagetian framework of logical thinking and 'the possibility of performance rather than competence problems in adult reasoning. The need to develop more effective instructional techniques to enhance transfer of learning was underscored', (*ibid.*, p. 255). (Details follow.) (Further training studies with respect to formal operational reasoning have received attention in Volume 3, in the present series, *Piagetian Research*).

k. Effects of Modelling upon Operativity

Sullivan (1967) attempted to accelerate operational thought through a filming technique. Four groups were formed: (a) Film modelling — verbal principle; (b) film modelling — no verbal principle; (c) natural conservers; and (d) a control group. The difference between the (a) and (b) conditions was that in the (a) condition, the intuitive observer heard a model produce a conservation judgment and justification while in the (b) condition, the model produced a conservation judgment only. Significantly more (a) (84 per cent) and (b) (76 per cent) than (d) subjects (10 per cent) showed operativity on the post-test.

In continuation, Sullivan (1969) aimed to measure the effects of amounts of training upon inducement, generalization and extinction post-tests. The (a) group viewed the modelling film once and the second (a) group viewed it three times. Likewise, one (b) group viewed a modelling film once and a second group viewed it three times. No significant differences between Ss viewing the one or three film sessions were computed. Moreover, contrary to the 1967 study results, the (a) Ss in each group performed at the higher levels than their (b) counterparts on all three post-test phases. In the second 1969 experiment the effects of the order of the three-phase post-test presentation and the time interval between the training and post-tests were measured. There were no significant differences between the (b), (a) and (d) subjects. These results were therefore contrary to the 1967 and the first 1969 experiments. Waghorn and Sullivan (1970) reported results identical to the Sullivan (1967) study.

Beilin (1965), has pointed to a limitation in the effectiveness of a verbal model: there was no generalization to nontrained properties. He concluded that, 'some element beyond verbal model training was necessary for "full" conservation, which no other training procedure is able to provide either, but which is achieved in less formal learning settings', p. 337. Beilin found that a large proportion of Ss who could conserve number and length without training could also conserve area.

In comparison, Ss who received verbal instruction (or two other training procedures) showed little or no generalization to the concept of area. However, Silverman and Stone (1972) argued that, 'Sullivan . . . included a condition in which the adult model gave conservation answers but did not give explanations in terms of conservation principles. While most subjects in this condition acquired and even generalized the conservation response, only a small proportion of them could justify their answers with a conservation principle. It would therefore appear that contradiction by another person cannot by itself account for the present findings in that the interaction experience served to induce conservation explanations as well as conservation answers', p. 607.

Strauss (1972) 'reviewed and interpreted the literature of experimental studies whose purposes were to determine rules of generation that transform a child's cognitive organization at one stage of development into that of the next, more advanced stage. The categories of the research methodology were consistent with the organismic—developmental approach, and the findings of the studies tended to support most of the hypotheses generated from this approach'. (Details follow later.)

Kuhn (1972) investigated the mechanisms in terms of which the developmental transformation from one cognitive structure to another occurs. 'An equilibration model of change (Piaget, 1967)' was contrasted with an alternative, imitation model. An experiment was presented in which it was attempted to 'induce change by presenting three- to eight-year-old children with experimental models, the structure of which reflects differing degrees of relationship to the child's own, previously assessed structural level. (Details follow later.) In continuation, Kuhn (1973) amended earlier reviews of imitation theory and research (e.g. Flanders, 1968) in which the Piagetian perspective was omitted. Piaget approaches imitation as one form of overall cognitive functioning, rather than as a special mechanism for the acquisition of novel responses. 'Consideration of this point of view provides the basis for a re-examination of the empirical imitation literature. Emphasized are: (a) the interaction of the child's cognitive structure and the structural characteristics of the model, and (b) the child's interpretation of the modelling stimulus and the experimental imitation situation'. (Details follow later.)

Children aged two- and three-years-old who were non-operational on a set of geometric stimuli according to complete similarity on a pre-test were categorized into three experimental conditions — the modelling condition being one of these (Denney and Acito, 1974). 'After the training sessions, the Ss were given two post-tests — one with stimuli identical to those used during the training session and one with a different set of geometric stimuli. On the post-tests, significantly more similarity classifications were obtained in the modelling condition. It was concluded that two- and three-year-olds can learn to group according to similarity'.

Modelling by exemplification and instruction in training conservation was studied by Rosenthal and Zimmerman (1972). 'Observational learning by middle class Anglo-Americans, by economically disadvantaged Chicano first graders, and by four-year-olds was found on multidimensional conservation tasks. Without further training, imitative conservation was generalized to new stimuli. Verbally praising the model's responses did not affect performance. A non-conserving model reduced initially conserving children's scores. A nonmodelling instructions procedure did not alter conservation. Providing a rule to explain stimulus equivalence improves responses when both judged equivalence and explanation were required, but not when judged equivalence alone was required. Observing a model conserve without giving explanations increased correct judgments plus rule responses in imitation, indicative of inferential thinking elicited by modelling', p. 392. (Details follow later.) In continuation, the effects of a model's grouping strategy and explanations were examined in three-, four-, and five-year-old children by Zimmerman (1974). Short observation of the model was effective in creating significant generalization and retention of a size-dimension grouping strategy. The model's explanations significantly helped acquisition. However, incentives failed to facilitate operativity. The S's CA influenced performance; three- and four-year-old Ss who were subjected to a model's size-dimension grouping responses were unable to group stimuli according to an initially used object-identity dimension. Both dimensions were used by the five-year-olds. On the other hand, a training procedure in which the model grouped according to both stimulus dimensions did induce four-year-olds successfully to employ both grouping strategies simultaneously. (Details follow.)

Using social-learning methods, Rosenthal and Zimmerman (1972) were able to show learning and generalization of multidimensional conservation tasks, using much shorter observational techniques, restricted to a single training session. 'In their research, a number of features, imposed by design constraints, require mention: (a) Although six diverse conservation dimensions were included in their training and transfer items, correct response always required a judgment (or judgment plus explanation) of stimulus equality, because only equal stimulus members were presented and transformed. (b) The children's answers were always given verbally; generalization was never tested with a task reflecting nonverbal evidence of conservation. (c) Retention after delay was not studied', Zimmerman and Rosenthal, (1974, p. 260).

These authors therefore examined the effects of modelling and corrective feedback on the conservation of equalities and inequalities 'with items spanning three stimulus dimensions (length, number, and two-dimensional space). Brief observation of a model, briefer correction training (joining positive feedback with verbal rule provision), and the combination of observation and correction were all successful in producing learning and, without further training, transfer and retention of conservation. Unlike the controls (who also never correctly answered any equality items), the trained, experimental groups gave evidence of spontaneously generalizing their new learning to a task that required nonverbal behaviour to manifest conservation,' p. 260. (Details of the study appear later.)

To examine the effects of modelling procedures in changing the questioning strategies of elderly people, Denney and Denney (1974) tested 42 white middle class adults between the ages of 70 and 90 who asked no constraint-seeking questions on a pre-test. In their 1973 study the authors found that compared to middle-aged women, elderly women ask more hypothesis-testing questions and fewer constraint-seeking questions. The 1974 Ss were divided into three experimental groups: an exemplary modelling condition, a cognitive-strategy modelling condition, and a control condition. In all three conditions, four 20-item arrays of pictures were employed as stimuli. 'During both modelling conditions, the Ss and the E took turns trying to guess which picture the other was thinking of. In the exemplary modelling condition, the E simply asked constraint-seeking questions when he was guessing; while in the cognitive-strategy modelling condition, the E verbalized his strategy for formulating and using his constraint-seeking questions in addition to exemplifying such questions. In the control condition, the S alone tried to guess which picture the E was thinking of; the E did not take turns with him. Following training, the Ss were presented with a post-test . . . Ss in both the exemplary modelling and cognitive-strategy modelling conditions asked significantly more constraint-seeking questions than the Ss in the control condition. There was no difference between the two modelling conditions in the percentage of constraint-seeking questions asked on the post-test, although the Ss in the cognitive-strategy modelling condition asked significantly more novel . . . constraint-seeking questions. The increase in the use of constraint-seeking questions in the two modelling conditions were accompanied by a decrease in the number of questions required for solution to the post-test problems.' (Details follow.)

The effectiveness of short-term training on two communication tasks was assessed by Shantz and Wilson (1972) with children aged seven years six months. 'Twelve Ss were trained in trios for six sessions on tasks requiring complete description of a design for a listener to reproduce, and tasks requiring communication of critical information for a listener to discriminate the same design from a set. Roles of speaker, listener, and observer were alternated, followed by peer discussion. Compared with 12 control Ss, trained Ss at post-testing had significantly greater useful information and overall evaluation of messages, and showed a moderate transfer of skills', p. 693. (Details follow.)

Assessment and training of role-taking and referential communication skills in 125 institutionalized emotionally disturbed children was evaluated by Chandler, Greenspan and Barenboim (1974). On the basis of this screening process, 48 Ss who performed at the lower levels on these measures were assigned randomly to one of two experimental training programmes intended to remediate deficits in either role-taking or referential communication skills. 'As a group these institutionalized Ss were found to be delayed significantly in the acquisition of both role taking and referential communication when compared with samples of their normal age-mates. Pre- and post-intervention comparisons indicated that Ss of both experimental groups improved significantly in their role-taking ability. Ss of the communication training programme also demonstrated significant improvement in referential communication skills. A 12-month follow-up showed a trend for improvements in both test measures to be associated with improvements in social adjustment as rated by institutional staff'. (Details follow.)

The study of Harris (1974) was concerned with the effectiveness of training prerequisite skills within the context of area conservation, in which subject verbalization was stressed via role-taking on performance of Piagetian tasks. 'The pre-test—post-test control group design was used in a five phase experiment: assessment of prerequisite skills, assessment of possession of conservation concepts via the Concept Assessment Kit — Conservation (Goldschmid and Bentler, 1968b), individualized training, first post-test to determine effectiveness of training, and second post-test two months later to assess durability and generalizability of training effects', p. 4869—A. Forty non-conserving white kindergarten Ss were assigned to control and experimental groups. All experimental Ss were trained to specified criterion levels. Twenty-two criterion tasks were interspersed within the first five training sessions in order to assess effectiveness of training. Training related to the concept of area conservation was successful for Ss ready to move into the operational stage of cognitive development. Training demonstrated both durability and generalization and the act of reversibility was observed as an important basic element in training. (Details follow.)

Conclusion

A diversity of opinion exists on how adequate the training procedures in the above studies have been. Inhelder (1969) argues that cognitive learning depends very much on the level at which the child is when interviewed. Inhelder cites a conservation experiment in which she offered training to completely pre-operational children and found that the great majority (87.5 per cent) did not make any real progress, while a minority (12.5 per cent) attained an intermediate level. The situation was rather different for those children who performed at the intermediate stage. 'Of the latter group, only 25 per cent made no progress at all but as for all the others, 75 per cent benefited from the learning procedures in varying degrees. For half of the latter group — 38 per cent — the acquisition of the conservation concept was no more than an extension of the structuration that had already begun at the time of the pre-test. But for the other half, true, progressive elaboration took place of which it is easy to follow the successive moments of integration during the learning sessions. So it is not that children learn nothing, but really it depends very much on their developmental level — the integration that is going on' (Inhelder and Sinclair, 1969).

Strauss and Langer (1970) argue that 'the Inhelder and Sinclair (1969) study was missing a crucial control condition to partial out repeated trials which might have revealed that the observed change in their transition Ss was not due to training. Rather, it may at least in part, be due to increased familiarity with the examiners and the testing procedures (*cf.* Zigler and Butterfield, 1968)'. The conclusions of Inhelder and Sinclair and Strauss and Langer are important. If the S himself has some even rudimentary sense of the conflict, it may be possible to devise interventions that may heighten his awareness of this conflict. It is difficult to induce change, however, unless the S has spontaneously begun the transition.

An analysis of the foregoing studies reveal certain patterns, the success of which might depend on: (a) the child's level of development at the beginning of training, (b) the training method employed, (c) the particular tasks used, (d) the amount of training, and (e) the criteria used to evaluate success.

The field of training efforts in concept inducement is a complex one and with greater sophistication in research techniques the researchers have tended to modify their original thinking. In this respect, Smedslund (1966) has modified the position he held (at the time of his 1961a study), that is a conversion from 'organism—object conflict' to organism—organism conflict', (1966). This shift in Smedslund's thinking in fact now renders it identical rather than similar to Piaget's.

Kohlberg (1968) in summing up the aspect of 'acceleration' comments that children who have conserved 'naturally' are more likely to generalize to other conservation tasks, whereas the effects of specific instruction or artificial acceleration seem to have limited generalization to other areas of conservation with the possibility of regression in conservation suggesting 'pseudo' rather than genuine conservation.

Numerous learning experiments that aimed to teach operational behavioural schemes have been reviewed by Beilin (1971, pp. 81—124), and Montada (1970). 'Although a variety of experimental techniques has been used — induction of cognitive conflicts, reversibility training, mobility training, verbal training, acquisition of learning sets (behaviouristic approach), multiple training methods, etc. — success in introducing operations has been obtained in most experiments, although not within each one of the diverse tests. Even verbal methods have led to success, although the Genevans emphatically assert and — for particular circumstances — have proved that verbal measures do not contribute much to the construction of cognitive structures (Sinclair-de-Zwart, 1969, pp. 315—336). It is paradoxical, however, that the Genevans, who make extensive use of the clinical method for uncovering the child's structure of thinking, have systematically minimized the importance of verbal interactions with the child for the construction of operational structures', (Montada, *op. cit.*, p. 895).

Inhelder (cited in Green, Ford and Flamer (Eds.), 1971, objects to the artificial dissociation of reversibility, compensation and identity for experimental purposes. She further maintains (and justifiably), that a comprehension of conservation as a whole necessitates the development of numerous interrelated processes, '. . . so if you accentuate (deliberately or accidentally) one aspect at the expense of others, you sometimes have distortions and later on there may even be a kind of breakdown'. However, while such an argument is sound and logical, the need for objectivity in research necessitates selection among the many areas that might be explored.

Wallace (1972) makes out a case for the active investigation of acceleration due to the possible advantages it might have for the intellectual development and education of retarded children and is convinced, despite Piaget's contention, that environmental demands should not be left to dictate the course of cognitive development.

Piaget (1972), commenting on stage acceleration, states that all education is just an acceleration, 'but it remains to be decided to what extent it is beneficial. It is not without significance that it takes man much longer to reach maturity than the other animals. Consequently, it is highly probable that there is an optimum rate of development, to exceed or fall behind which would be equally harmful. But we do not know its laws, and on this point as well it will be up to future research to enlighten us'.

Kuhn (1974) has made several suggestions for improvement of the training study as a method of research in developmental psychology. '. . . it is suggested that every training study should be undertaken as a part of a research programme that has as its foundation a careful longitudinal assessment of the natural development of that concept and any concepts thought to be closely related which are to be studied experimentally . . . Assessment would begin at an age when some or all of the assessed behaviours were just beginning to appear and would continue throughout the period of development until all Ss exhibited all behaviours . . . Such data would enable us to know (a) the length of time the development being studied naturally takes and (b) most important, the patterns of development across the various behaviours involved . . . After (this) initial assessment, interventions that it was thought might induce progress could be introduced. Natural history data might potentially become useful at this point in a second way — as a source of ideas for interventions likely to be successful . . . An intervention would at first be introduced only on a single occasion at some given point in the subject's developmental history . . . the most appropriate point for initial experimentation with intervention is during the subject's transitional stage . . . In subsequent experiments, the number, frequency, and duration of intervention sessions would gradually be increased . . . the interventions would be spaced out over the period that the development in question normally occurs . . . Each attempt at intervention, varying in number, duration, or frequency of sessions, would constitute a separate experiment, requiring the appropriate post-test assessments . . . the strategy might be viewed as an attempt to discover how slowly, rather than how rapidly, we can accelerate development, still preserving its natural characteristics . . . Attempting to approximate the natural developmental process as closely as possible should bring us closer to what is the most worthy objective of training studies, understanding this process itself', pp. 598–600.

Recently, Inhelder, Sinclair and Bovet (1974) have focused on the question as to whether experiments on learning have a place within the psychological and epistemological framework. The authors believe that work on learning is not only compatible with developmental psychology, but that it may help to overcome some of the difficulties encountered in cognitive learning theories: 'All theories of learning are constructed from postulates about the nature of knowledge and hypotheses on cognitive development. There have been many recent attempts to adapt what are

basically stimulus-response theories of learning to the increasing complexity of experimental findings, but they may in fact be impossible if the
difficulties turn out to be inherent in the fundamental epistemological
tenets of such theories'. One of the main problems dealt with by the
authors is the study of the transition from one stage of cognitive development to the next through investigations into the mechanisms that promote the growth of knowledge. Previous Genevan research having
clarified the concept of developmental stages, the major concern of their
work was to discover 'the processes of integration that result in novel
types of behaviour', studied by means of 'a method based on learning'.

The authors commenced with the idea that under certain conditions an
acceleration of cognitive development would be possible, 'but that this
could only occur if the training procedures in some way resembled the
kind of situations in which progress takes place outside an experimental
set-up'. They considered that if such training procedures could be
constructed, it would then be possible to analyse both the favourable
conditions and the children's reactions and thereby to observe in some
detail 'the different transitions and the dynamics of progress'. They
were guided by what is already known about general trends in
development and about the types of difficulties young children
encounter when trying to reason about problems presented, namely:
cognitive development results essentially from interaction between the
subject and his environment, together with the stimulation of
intellectual activity from opportunities for acting, observing other
people's actions or for discussion corresponding to the subject's level of
development. Further, that training procedures should take into
account the fact that new structures are formed through the integration
and coordination of already existing schemes. 'This idea that schemes
or preconcepts should be coordinated and integrated to new structures
links up with another point, which is that of the existence of necessary
stages of development. This hypothesis implies the existence of certain
major paths leading to the acquisition of knowledge. Training
procedures should steer the subject in the right direction, even if this
results temporarily in incorrect reasoning. Variations are, however,
possible, and it is certainly not true that for each acquisition there is
only one predetermined construction process'.

On the basis of the above understanding, experimental stituations
were designed in order to elicit the use of the different modes of
reasoning expected to play a part in the various concepts investigated.
The main goal was to get a better insight into the transition (or
construction) mechanisms within the realms of conservation (numerical, physical and spatial) and their derivations, together with the
concept of quantification of class-inclusion and its eventual links with
conservation of quantity. Children were presented with a range of

problems, each calling for a different scheme, with the intention of arousing a conflict in the child's mind 'between these schemes that would lead to new types of coordination between them'. Subjects who were on the verge of acquiring the concept were eliminated, but selection criteria did not take into account differences in s.e.s., degree of schooling or in IQ. Pre-tests included detailed questioning allowing the division of the subjects into several groups according to their level and at least one task dealing with a closely related notion, generally one acquired at the same age. Post-tests, satisfied the requirements of consisting of two, in order to check the stability of the process; were more stringent replications of pre-tests; included at least one problem involving material different from that used in the pre-tests and training procedures and included a question requiring a type of answer different from those called for by the pre-tests and training, together with a problem whose solution requires a notion related, but not identical to that treated during the training.

The authors report that the results bore out the assumption that only if training procedures are effective can the acquisition processes at work in the individual child be observed. Cognitive development was accelerated, providing many opportunities for observing transitional behaviours. In counteraction the design of the training procedures indicated disagreement with classical learning theorists. The nature and extent of the subjects' progress was always dependent upon their initial developmental level; once the subjects showed a clear understanding of a conservation or class-inclusion concept this remained stable, 'by contrast, many of the subjects who at the first post-test reached one of the intermediate levels either regressed or progressed at the second post-test.' However, 'The comparison of pre-tests and post-tests of all our experiments taken together leads to the conclusion that the findings fit the conception of learning as an integral part of the developmental mechanisms'. Additional evidence for confirmation of the Genevan view that semilogical constructs are inherent in the child's thought and necessary for his progress was provided, in contradiction of the Galperin school that inadequate modes of reasoning are, in the main, artifacts caused by insufficient and incorrect education. (Full discussion of the results can be found in Inhelder *et al.*, 1974.) In conclusion the authors summarize that 'learning is a constantly renewed process of synthesis between continuity and novelty'.

Piaget (1974) in comment states that the importance of the results lies in the discovery that all the observed modifications of thought patterns consist either in developmental accelerations or in conflicts. Development cannot be reduced to a series of bits of learning and 'the notion of competence has to be introduced as a precondition for any learning to take place'. Piaget emphasizes that the authors are right in refusing to draw general conclusions concerning the value of other training methods: 'In my opinion, three questions remain open as regards the theoretical implications of the various results of these different training methods. First — and it is surprising that this problem has been so rarely discussed — one must ask whether the progress obtained is stable or whether, like many things learned in school, it disappears with time. Second, one must determine whether the observed accelerations are accompanied by deviations from the general development trend. Certain educational experiments concerning didactic methods of teaching the quantification of class-inclusion have been repeated by psychologists, who have shown that such training may result in a disturbance of the subject's understanding of the relationship between the complementary classes A and A'. The final and most important question concerns the necessity of checking whether progress obtained independently from natural development can serve as a basis for new spontaneous constructions or whether the subject who passively receives information from the adult will no longer learn anything without such help, as was so often the case with traditional methods of education. The importance of the training methods described in this book lies in the fact that the subject's creative capacities are encouraged rather than suppressed'.

Bolton (1975) in reviewing Inhelder, Sinclair and Bovet (*op. cit.*) maintained that the '. . . book is addressed to what has perhaps been the greatest weakness in Piaget's theory of intellectual development. The description of the stages of development remains an enormous and solid achievement, well able to incorporate local criticism such as those made by Bruner and Bryant. But the theory has never satisfactorily explained the transition from one stage of intelligence to the next, the concept of "equilibration" or cognitive conflict appearing as no more than suggestive of a possible type of explanation rather than being adequate in itself. Inhelder and her colleagues go a long way in this account in overcoming this problem, the closeness and lucidity of their analysis begins to reveal the nature of the transitional process, the sorts of cognitive involved and the ways in which they promote development, in a much more concrete way than hitherto. Inhelder relates that the studies reported in this volume grew out of a collaboration with Bruner at Harvard. The findings of the "Harvard School" are reported in Bruner, Olver and Greenfield's *Studies in Cognitive Growth* (Wiley, 1966). *Learning and the Development of Cognition* is the equivalent volume from the Geneva School and contains fundamental criticisms of Bruner's interpretations. The authors are of the opinion that several of the experiments conducted by Bruner and his colleagues train the child to give correct answers in a specific situation rather than developing genuine operational structures. They insist, for example, that different situations must be presented for the evaluation of the child's understanding of a concept and that it is not sufficient for the child to give but one justification for conservation since this may express only a partial coordination of operational structures: instead the child should be encouraged to give several arguments (reversibility, compensation, and identity) so that the experiments can assess the "degree of completion" of the child's operational schemes', pp. 1073–1074.

Abstracts

The development of time concepts through conflict based on a primitive duration capacity
T.J. Berndt and D.J. Wood, 1974

AIM / The development of time concepts through conflict based on a primitive duration capacity was investigated.

SUBJECTS / N = 40. Half the subjects were aged five and the other half seven years.

METHOD / 'The apparatus comprised red and blue toy electric train engines five inches long. The parallel tracks were four feet long and four inches apart. A tunnel which could be lowered to cover both tracks, held two speakers connected to a stereo tape recorder — whenever the red train was running, a 220-H tone sounded. A 750-H tone sounded when the blue train was running. The tunnel was arranged over the track so that, when the trains were in the starting position, they could be seen resting against parallel stops', p. 826.
Pre-test. Two standard Piagetian tests were administered before the training sessions, patterned after Piaget (1969).
Training. 'While a single train was running, the child was asked to identify it by listening to its whistle. After his reply, and with the train still whistling, the tunnel was raised and any error was pointed out to him. This procedure was repeated with both trains in random order until the child made five successive correct identifications', p. 826. The training phase comprised three parts, details of which are described elsewhere, Berndt and Wood, (1974, p. 826).

RESULTS / The authors conclude, 'Children made accurate duration judgments when using only auditory cues (whistles), indicating that a primitive capacity for judging duration exists. When visual and auditory cues were available, children tended to use a distance model, that is, longer distance = longer time. The children experienced conflict when an initial choice based on auditory cues was shown to be incompatible with the distance model. Various attempts to resolve this conflict were compared. Some solutions seemed to indicate development toward operational time concepts. The results were contrasted with Piaget's (1969) theory of the development of time concepts, and the usefulness of the method in diagnosis of cognitive development was discussed', p. 825.

Changes in logical thinking as a function of induced disequilibrium
M.D. Berzonsky, T.P. Lombardo, and M.A. Ondrako, 1975

AIM / To induce disequilibrium in subjects responding with systematic logical errors, to conditional logic problems.

SUBJECTS / N = 67 introductory psychology students.

METHOD / The logic tests were constructed from items used by Roberge (1971, p. 339). The four tests: pre-test, experimental or control treatment, post-test, and dogmatism scale were contained in one booklet. The control and experimental booklets were mixed together and randomly given to the Ss. The experimental condition involved solving logic syllogisms when the obvious 'logical error' was not included as a possible answer. Control Ss solved the same problems with the 'logical error' included as a choice. (Fuller details of the material used and experimental procedures adopted are given in Berzonsky, Lombardo, and Ondrako, 1975, pp 256–257.)

RESULTS / Subjects' pre-test—post-test enhancement scores demonstrate that the experimental group did significantly better than the control group on invalid principles, by a relatively short-term treatment designed to induce disequilibrium and changes in the subjects' reasoning strategies. 'These effects appear to support the view that adult difficulties with conditional reasoning problems — at least those invalid problems employed in the . . . study . . . reflect, at least in part, a performance rather than competence difference. The need to develop more effective instructional methods designed to facilitate transfer of learning was underscored. If, in fact, the problems that adults experience with logic problems are performance rather than competency based, such results would seem readily reconcilable with Piaget's theory of logical thinking', (*ibid.*, p. 260).

Classification and seriation instruction and logical task performance in the preschool
A.M. Bingham-Newman and F.H. Hooper, 1974

AIM / To explicate the role of instructional experiences (seriation, classification, combined seriation/classification) as determinants of performance on Piagetian tasks in young children.

SUBJECTS / N = 60 aged three years four months to five years nine months.

METHOD / 'In view of the recognized self-instructional effect of repeated Piagetian task administrations, a variation of the Solomon four-group design (Campbell and Stanley, 1963) was employed. This permitted the evaluation of potential pre-testing or pre-test/treatment interaction effects. Two training groups for each treatment condition (one pre-tested and one nonpre-tested group) were arranged for each pre-school location. In addition, one control group was assigned to Pre-school A and two control groups to Pre-school B. Each group consisted of four, approximately age matched, children. Twelve children from the Pre-school A morning group were randomly assigned, four per group to the three training conditions. Sixteen children from the Pre-school A afternoon group were randomly assigned to three training conditions and one control group. Each of the classrooms in Pre-school A was already a mixed age group. The classrooms in Pre-school B were grouped by age. To mix ages and yet not isolate any child from familiar peers, pairs of children from each class were randomly assigned to groups. The resulting groups of four were then randomly assigned, two groups each, to the three training conditions and the control groups', Bingham-Newman and Hooper (1974, p. 381).

The seriation training sessions followed those in Hooper (1972) with minor modification. The ten training sessions followed the sequence: comparison between two sizes; relative comparison; successive comparison; serial correspondence; additive seriation; multiple seriation. The classification training sessions followed the sequence: resemblance sorting; consistent sorting; exhaustive sorting; some and all; dual class membership; and whole is the sum of its parts. The sequence was patterned after Kofsky (1966).

The assessment measures included the Peabody Picture Vocabulary Test (Form B); Relational terms task (Griffiths, Shantz, and Sigel, 1967); Seriation tasks (Elkind, 1964; Coxford, 1964; Shantz and Sigel, 1967); Classification tests (Kofsky, 1966; Shantz and Sigel, 1967); Number conservation (Rothenberg 1969); and Conservation of surface area (Piaget, Inhelder, and Szeminska 1960).

RESULTS / Significant specific transfer effects were computed for the seriation instructional condition. However, little differences were noted for the classification, verbal intelligence, and for transfer conservation task measures. Sex differences, school location effects, teacher biases, and pre-testing effects were generally not present. 'The apparent feasibility of seriation skill instruction for pre-school aged children and the general non-effectiveness of the classificatory and combined instructional conditions, particularly insofar as transfer effects are concerned, suggests a nonunitary picture of cognitive functioning during the transitionary phases between operational and concrete operations period thought', p. 379.

The effects of instruction in the concept of speed and proportions on children in the third grade
F.D. Boulanger, 1974

AIM / The author was intent to investigate the effects of systematic instruction in the concept of speed and proportions on the performance of concrete operational subjects.

SUBJECTS / N = 51 children from third grade.

METHOD / A screening test selected a sample of children capable of performing simple division and demonstrated operativity on time, speed and spatial concepts. Two instructional and a control group were established. 'The training and comparison treatment was a sequence of problems, questions, and demonstrations interwoven with training in the concept of speed and simple proportions. The comparison only treatment was the same sequence of problems, questions, and demonstrations but without training in the concept of speed and simple proportions. All instruction in both treatments was done on an individual basis. The control group received no instruction dealing with speed and proportions. Three dependent measures were administered on an immediate and on a delayed basis. Immediately after the completion of instruction, children in the treatment groups were individually administered measures of retention, transfer, and transfer to two Piagetian tasks. Three weeks later, three similar measures were administered again individually. The control group children were individually administered the same measures . . . the same times as the treatment group children'.

RESULTS / The data were subjected to the analysis of variance techniques. Subjects in the training and comparison treatment group performed at the higher levels when compared to the control group on the immediate retention measure. However, this was not true on the delayed retention measure. No significant differences were computed among the three groups on either the immediate transfer measure or the delayed transfer measure. The control group scored significantly higher than subjects in the training and comparison group on the immediate administration of Piagetian task two. However, this was not upheld with the delayed administration of the same task. Although training tended to induce a speed comparison task, it lacked both transfer and durability.

Training and transfer of transitivity, conservation, and class inclusion of length
C.J. Brainerd, 1974

AIMS / The main objectives were formulated as follows:

(a) 'Is it possible to induce durable and minimally general improvements in transitivity, conservation, and class-inclusion by providing positive-negative feedback that is contingent upon children's judgments'?
(b) 'Given a single training procedure of proven effectiveness, are transitivity, conservation, and class inclusion differentially susceptible to training'?
(c) 'Does experimentally induced transitivity or conservation or class inclusion transfer to either or both of the other two indexes of concrete operations'?
(d) 'Does interconcept transfer of training occur for any of the three indexes'?
(e) 'Assuming that there is interconcept transfer, is the amount of transfer the same for all three indexes'?

SUBJECTS / N = 144, with an age-range from four years five months to five years six months.

METHOD / The pre-tests included: transitivity of length, transitivity of weight, conservation of length, conservation of weight, class inclusion of length, class inclusion of weight and an understanding of the relational terms. The tests were patterned after Brainerd (1973a, 1973b). Fuller details are also described in Brainerd (1974, pp. 326–328).
Training — Each of the 144 subjects was assigned to one of the treatment conditions: (a) Transitivity training, (b) Transitivity control,

(c) Conservation, (d) Conservation control, (e) Class-inclusion training and, (f) Class-inclusion control. Full details of the training trials appear in Brainerd (1974, p. 329).

Post-tests were administered one week after the training trials. These were identical to the pre-tests.

RESULTS / With regard to hypothesis (a) above, feedback manipulation facilitated performance in transitivity, conservation, and class inclusion which were 'both durable and minimally general'. With respect to hypothesis (b) above, transitivity, conservation, and class inclusion were differentially responsive to training. Concerning hypothesis (c) above, 'it was noted earlier that Piaget's *structures d'ensemble* postulates for concrete operations leads one to anticipate substantial transfer of training among transitivity, conservation, and class inclusion.' The post-test data provided no support for this prediction. There was no evidence that either conservation training or class-inclusion training transfers to the other two skills. Some slight transfer of transitivity training to length conservation was observed. With respect to hypothesis (d) post-test data provided evidence of interconcept transfer of training for all three skills. Concerning hypothesis (e) above, varied amounts of interconcept transfer were noted for transitivity, conservation, and class inclusion.

Acquisition and generalization of conservation by pre-schoolers, using operant training
B. Bucher and R.E. Schneider, 1973

AIMS / The authors formulated two objectives: '. . . to develop a conditional discrimination learning method to train children under age five to conserve number, and to extend training to conservation of substance and liquid quantity . . . The secondary aim . . . was to examine two procedural features that may have introduced artifacts into previous number conservation training studies that have used feedback; and to assess the effects of these biases and eliminate them by appropriate training', p. 188.

SUBJECTS / N = 32 within the age range from three years one month to five years.

METHOD / Two main training phases were administered: training to judge the relative numerical sizes of two rows of objects (Number Relations Training); followed by training in conservation of number, substance and liquid quantity. Each Conservation training step comprised reinforced trials continuing until criterion was reached. 'Test trials were then interpolated between further training trials, to test for transfer to the next step or to assess the influence of a source of response bias', p.190. (Details of the training phases and testing procedures are described in Bucher and Schneider, 1973, pp. 190–194.)

RESULTS / The authors conclude, '... results indicate that children generally thought to be well below the stage at which conservation is normally seen can be trained to judge conserving and non-conserving transformations successfully, and can master an increasing variety of problems with little additional training. Training successfully induced discrimination between conserving and non-conserving transformations for over half the children studied, for three quantitative characteristics. Most unsuccessful subjects dropped out during Number Relations Training. Subjects who dropped out during Conservation Training were performing with average accuracy in all but one case. The average entering age of children who completed training was four years two months, which did not differ significantly from the age of those who dropped out', p. 198. Bucher and Schneider continue, 'It is concluded that conservation training studies have frequently failed to control for possible artifacts that can produce false positive responding. In examining the present successful training, it is concluded that operant training programmes show considerable potential for developing behaviour skills indicative of conservation, even in pre-operational children. More detailed analysis of the behavioural manifestations of conservation is needed before it can be determined whether such training actually induces conservation as a cognitive ability', p. 187.

Training in logical thinking and its effects on the grouping strategies of eight-year-old children
E. Burke, 1974

AIM / To investigate the effects of training in symbolic logic on the grouping strategies of young children.

SUBJECTS / N = 60 children aged eight years. Subjects were randomly assigned to an experimental and control group, each group comprising 12 boys and 18 girls.

METHOD / The teaching programme employed was Furth's Symbolic Logic Programme (Furth, 1970) 'which focuses on the

comprehension of logical symbols for affirmation, negation, con-
junction and disjunction in symbolic expressions, together with
subsequent application of these expressions. In all cases the problem
presented consists of three parts, a symbolic expression (H,S, T or A), a
picture of what is symbolized (picture of house, sun, tree, or apple)
and, between the two, an arrow (possibly crossed) indicating whether
the picture is or is not an instance of the expression . . . The subjects
had to indicate whether the symbolic expression and the instance
match, or to supply an instance of the expression. The programme is
largely nonverbal in that the stimulated responses involve little
connected language. It would thus seem reasonable to assume that
subjects with a restricted language code would not be penalized',
pp. 305–306.

Subjects in the experimental group received training on the
programme for nine consecutive weeks. (Fuller details of the
Programme are also described in Burke, 1974, pp. 305–307.) At the
end of the training subjects were administered criterion tasks of
equivalence formation with verbal and pictorial materials. These were
adapted from Bruner *et. al.* (1966).

RESULTS / The data were subjected to a three-way analysis of
variance. 'Generally the training was found to be beneficial for the
boys, but not for the girls, the training x sex interaction being
significant for performance in the verbal test. Again, for both tests,
more of the experimental group displayed above-average groupings in the
functional and nominal categories, the difference from the controls
being statistically significant', p. 311. The study concludes by
discussing the usefulness or otherwise of conducting acceleration
studies.

*Effects of testing conditions on Piaget matrices and order of appearance
problems: a study of competence vs performance**
J.S. Carlson and R. Dillon, 1976

The presence or absence of a correct response to a task presented in
a psychological assessment situation is usually taken as an indication of
the presence or absence of the capability under study. Since it is
possible for negative, incorrect responses to be due to factors such as
lack of understanding or misunderstanding of the question and task

* Published with the kind permission of the authors. Gratitude is extended to
Professor Jerry S. Carlson and Dr Ronna Dillon of the University of California,
Riverside.

demands, forgetting, etc., Type II error is possible. Type I error may occur if correct solution is obtained through faulty means such as by guessing, irrelevant procedures, etc. The correctness or incorrectness of the symptom response may lead to false negatives or false positives and misinterpretations of the presence or absence of the capability under study (Smedslund, 1969). Beyond this and the focal point of this investigation, however, is the problem of accurately assessing a capability that is present or in the process of consolidation but not activated. This issue is of special importance to cognitive theories which employ the use of constructs such as schemes or structures. Flavell and Wohlwill (1969) point out, for example, the appropriateness of the competence-performance distinction in studying Piaget developmental phenomena. The cognitive viewpoint stresses that one must know a great deal about the particular concepts being tested and the abilities and strategies of the child in order to determine the degree to which performance accurately reflects, or even accurately approaches what the 'true' competence is.

Studies dealing with the relationship between cognitive competence and performance in normal children point to the general conclusion that performance levels under particular conditions are often less than perfect indicators of capacity (Birch and Bortner, 1966; Clarke, Clarke and Cooper, 1970). This position was supported and clarified in studies investigating the activation of existing but not fully activated cognitive structures through reduction of perceptual features of matrices (Overton and Brodzinsky, 1972) and spatial perspective (Brodzinsky, Jackson and Overton, 1972) tasks. The basic conclusion of these studies was that the reduction of perceptual features led to higher performance for transitional children but such manipulations did not affect performance for younger pre-operational children or for older children who were already at the level of concrete operational thought. It was suggested that already or nearly emerged structures were in the process of consolidation and for the transitional children were activated. Their performance was indicative of the level of competence they actually had but which may not have been tapped by a standard testing procedure.

An important aspect of the activation model (Overton, 1975) which should be stressed is that totally new structures are not formed or acquired for the first time during the testing period (*cf.* Aebli, 1961; Seiler, 1968), they are simply brought to use. The preponderance of evidence from various training studies on conservation supports this, as typically only children at transitional stages seem to be affected by the experimental manipulations (Beilin, 1971; Inhelder, Sinclair and Bovet, 1974). Thus, it might be concluded that activation is involved in training effects.

In 'testing-the-limits' terms, evidence indicates that feedback and verbalization yield better performance on tests such as *Raven's Progressive Matrices* (Carlson *et al.*, 1974; Guthke, 1972). Furthermore, these manipulations, as well as simple test repetition, produce significantly higher correlations of the test with various aspects of school achievement such as grades and teachers' judgments of potential than otherwise exist.

The main purpose of the present study was to investigate the issue of possibly varying levels of performance through the effects of testing procedure on two Piaget derived tasks of concrete operational thought and to relate the scores obtained to a variety of school achievement and achievement potential data. Transitional age children were selected as they are at the point where divergence between competence and performance, in the sense described, is most likely to be maximal. Subparts of a recently developed standardized test of cognitive development (Winkelmann, 1975) were used so that the standardized conditions could be compared with a condition designed to involve the child in active participation with the test materials in a manner similar to that of a school situation. Here, emphasis is placed on dialogue and interaction between the testor and testee so that a 'real life' situation is developed, one in which the child is not alienated. This is in keeping with a concern recently raised by Riegel (1975) that 'objective,' standardized approaches of test administration should be abandoned in favour of a type of situation which a child actually encounters in everyday life, one in which he is given feedback, is asked and can ask questions, and is helped to understand the salient features of the problem at hand. In addition to exploring the possible differences in performance in the standardized versus the nonstandardized condition, repetition of the tests under each condition after a three week period was done.

The main expectations of the study were that higher levels of performance on the Piaget measures would be detected in the nonstandardized as opposed to the standardized condition, as well as for the second as opposed to the first testing. In addition, it was expected that the Piaget measures would correlate more highly with school achievement and judged student potential in the nonstandard condition and on the repeated testing than for the standard condition and the first testings.

SUBJECTS / The subjects consisted of a total of 46 middle class children. All children were in the second grade. Their average age was seven years eight months, SD = 0.59. The Ss were randomly assigned to two testing conditions: standardized and nonstandardized. All Ss were tested twice, the second testing approximately three weeks after the first. Thus a 2 x 2 repeated measures design was employed. Males and females were equally represented in the sample.

MATERIALS / The Matrices and Order of Appearance subtests of a recently developed Piaget-derived test battery were used (Winkelmann, 1975). The Matrices test consists of eight items, each showing a stimulus array where horizontal and vertical dimensions are presented that vary consistently along given dimensions. The task for S is to find from a set of eight distractors the correct pattern that will complete the two dimensional array. The Order of Appearance test has 16 items. Each item shows a set of three differently coloured balls located in a 'house.' Attached to the house is a tube that varies in number of convolutions through which S is told to imagine that the balls will pass. His task is to select from a set of six distractors the correct picture of how the balls would look if they rolled from their original house to another at the end of the tube.

PROCEDURES / The Matrices and Order of Appearance tests were administered individually to all Ss. In the standard condition the procedures outlined by Winkelmann were followed. For the Matrices, S was shown the stimulus form and asked: 'Which of these figures belongs here?' After his response there was no feedback; testor–testee interaction was minimal. After S completed one task, the page was turned and he was once again asked which figure belongs in the empty space. Similarly, for Order of Appearance, a noninteractive approach was used. S was told, 'Here three balls roll along this path to their house. You are supposed to show me how they look when the balls are in their house. Which of these pictures is correct?'

The nonstandard condition used the same materials and the initial question for each task was as in the standard condition. But after S responded, he was given positive or negative feedback by E. If the reinforcement was positive, E asked S why he made the choice he did. This was followed by E picking up on this and repeating or expanding on why it was correct and pointing out the salient features involved. If S's response was incorrect and the reinforcement was negative, he was asked why he made the selection he did. Then it was pointed out to him why it was incorrect and he was again asked to choose the correct figure. When the correct selection had been made, E explained why it and only it is correct. In both instances of an initial correct or incorrect response, the specific nature of the dialogue between E and S depended on the task and statements which S might make or questions he or S might pose. Clearly the purpose here was not a standardized approach disregarding the specific situation. Thus although general guidelines operated as to the nature of the interaction, it varied from task to task and child to child.

The scoring of the standard and nonstandard conditions was the same. After the initial questions, which were the same for both conditions, the S's response was scored 1 if it was correct, 0 if it was incorrect. The time involved varied not only between conditions, but also within the nonstandardized condition. Normally, however, the total testing time was approximately 10 minutes for the standard condition and 20 minutes for the nonstandard condition.

School achievement and achievement potential measures were collected. Teachers' judgments of reading achievement, reading potential, math achievement and math potential were obtained for each child by means of the Q-sort technique. Scores on either the California Test of Basic Skills (CTBS) or the Wide Range Achievement Test (WRAT) were also obtained for each child. From these tests only math and reading achievement scores were used. All of the achievement data were standardized. The reliability of the four Q-sorts was determined by Hoyt's procedures and found to be .96.

RESULTS / The means and standard deviations for all measures of achievement and judgment of achievement and potential are reported in Table 1. Table 1 also shows the means and standard deviations for the two Piaget tests used, Matrices and Order of Appearance, for the two testing conditions, standard (A) and nonstandard (B), and the two times of test administration (T_1 and T_2).

Table 1: Means and standard deviations for all measures

Test and condition	Mean	SD
Matrices		
Standard (A) at T_1	2.04	1.92
Nonstandard (B) at T_1	4.30	1.69
Standard (A) at T_2	3.17	2.48
Nonstandard (B) at T_2	6.35	2.14
Order of Appearance		
Standard (A) at T_1	7.56	3.23
Nonstandard (B) at T_1	11.83	3.23
Standard (A) at T_2	8.96	3.12
Nonstandard (B) at T_2	14.26	1.89
Reading Achievement	51.84	8.20
Math Achievement	47.81	8.26
Reading Achievement Q-Sort	50.73	8.61
Reading Potential Q-Sort	51.48	8.54
Math Achievement Q-Sort	47.92	9.85
Math Potential Q-Sort	48.01	10.28

The data from the Piaget measures were subjected to two independent 2 x 2 repeated measures analyses of variance. Table 2 reports these
results for the Matrices test; Table 3 for the Order of Appearance test.
In both analyses, significant F values (p < .001) were calculated for
condition of test administration and for time of administration. The
significant main effects detected were in the direction of higher
performance in the nonstandardized as opposed to the standardized
conditions and on the second testings as opposed to the first. No
significant interactions between condition and time were detected for
either test although a trend toward interaction was detected for the
Matrices test (F = 2.68, df = 1 / 44, p = .10) where maximum gains
were shown in the nonstandard condition at time 2.

Table 2: ANOVA on matrices

Source	df	MS	F
Between Ss			
Conditions (C)	1	169.84	24.78*
Ss within groups	44	6.85	
Within Ss			
Time (T)	1	57.92	32.35*
C x T	1	4.79	2.68
Ss within groups x T	44	1.79	
Total	91		

* Significant p < .001.

Table 3: ANOVA on Order of Appearance

Source	df	MS	F
Between Ss			
Conditions (C)	1	526.08	40.41*
Ss within groups	44	13.02	
Within Ss			
Time (T)	1	84.17	19.75*
C x T	1	6.26	1.47
Ss within groups x T	44	4.26	
Total	91		

* Significant, p < .001.

Pearson product-moment correlations were calculated between the
Piaget tests under the various conditions and times and all of the
achievement measures. The results are reported in Table 4.

Table 4: Correlations between achievement and Piaget tasks given in standard (A) and Nonstandard (B) Conditions at Times 1 and 2 (n = 23)

| | Matrices | | | | Order of Appearance | | | |
| | T_1 Condition | | T_2 Condition | | T_1 Condition | | T_2 Condition | |
	A	B	A	B	A	B	A	B
Reading Ach.	.29	.20	.20	.31	.08	.23	.06	.31
Math Ach.	.56*	.35	.49*	.39*	.39*	.27	.31	.36
Reading Ach. Q	.29	.44*	.26	.54*	.08	.36	.23	.51*
Reading Pot. Q	.23	.40*	.16	.54*	−.05	.32	.15	.53*
Math Ach. Q	.37	.34	.40*	.42*	.27	.21	.25	.39*
Math Pot. Q	.37	.44*	.31	.53*	.01	.29	.06	.51*

* Significant, $p < .05$.

Inspection of the correlations shows that the Matrices test is not significantly correlated ($p > .05$) with the group reading test scores regardless of condition or time of test administration. Significant correlations ($p < .05$), on the other hand, were detected for all other achievement variables and the Matrices given under nonstandardized conditions at time 2 and the nonstandardized condition at time 1 except for Math Achievement Q. The only consistently significant ($p < .05$) correlations between Order of Appearance and the achievement measures involves the Q-sorts where teachers' judgments of achievement and potential were involved. These were detected only for the nonstandardized condition at time 2. Thus it appears that for both Piaget measures, maximum relationship between teachers' judgment of reading and math achievement or potential is obtained under the nonstandardized condition and on the second test administration.

Multiple regression was employed for analysis of comparison of the composite Piaget scores as dependent variables and the achievement variables as predictors. Stepdown procedures with Darlington's usefulness criteria were used. For the Matrices test, Reading Achievement Q-Sort was the only variable which approached statistical significance ($F = 3.23$, df = 1 / 41, $p < .10$). For the Order of Appearance test, the only statistically significant predictor ($F = 10.04$, df = 1 / 41, $p < .005$) was Math Potential Q-Sort.

Thus to determine if the various manipulations used in the Piaget measures were differentially related to the most salient predictors determined from the multiple regressions, analyses of variance procedures were used with high—low blocking on the predictor variable. Table 5 shows the means and standard deviations for the Matrices for a high—low block on Reading Achievement Q-Sort. Table 6 reports the results of the 2 x 2 x 2 ANOVA, with the two conditions A and B, two levels of Reading Q-Sort and repeated measures for T_1 and T_2.

Table 5: Means and standard deviations for matrices for high—low block on Reading Achievement Q-Sort

Condition	Mean		SD	
	High Group	Low Group	High Group	Low Group
Standard (A) at T_1	3.25	1.45	2.25	1.43
Nonstandard (B) at T_1	4.90	3.27	1.37	1.49
Standard (A) at T_2	4.37	2.36	2.77	1.91
Nonstandard (B) at T_2	7.55	5.27	2.33	0.69

Table 6: ANOVA for matrices test blocked on Reading Achievement Q-Sort

Source	df	MS	F
Between Ss			
Conditions (C)	1	114.82	22.3*
Reading Achievement (R)	1	74.84	14.5*
C x R	1	0.01	0.0
Ss within groups	37	5.15	
Within Ss			
Time (T)	1	55.74	36.85*
C x T	1	8.51	5.61**
R x T	1	0.91	0.60
C x R x T	1	0.22	0.15
T x Ss within groups	37	1.52	
Total	81		

* $p < .001$
** $p < .05$

Similar procedures were employed for the Order of Appearance test where the blocking variable was Math Potential Q-Sort. Table 7 reports the means and standard deviations. The results of the 2 x 2 x 2 ANOVA are given in Table 8.

Table 7: Means and standard deviations for Order of Appearance for high—low block on Math Potential Q-Sort

Condition	Mean		SD	
	High Group	Low Group	High Group	Low Group
Standard (A) at T_1	9.33	8.09	3.62	2.30
Nonstandard (B) at T_1	12.57	10.50	2.70	3.39
Standard (A) at T_2	10.33	8.90	3.33	2.66
Nonstandard (B) at T_2	15.57	13.00	.53	2.83

Table 8: ANOVA for Order of Appearance Test blocked on Math Potential Q-Sort

Source	df	MS	F
Between Ss			
Conditions (C)	1	197.75	19.49*
Math Pot. Q (MQ)	1	47.11	4.64**
C x MQ	1	3.44	.34
Ss within groups	26	10.15	
Within Ss			
Time (T)	1	47.22	9.78*
C x T	1	11.95	2.47
R x T	1	.41	.08
C x R x T	1	.09	.02
T x Ss within groups	26	4.83	
Total	59		

* $p < .01$
** $p < .05$

As was to be expected, for both analyses of variance main effects due to condition, time and the blocking variables were detected. These were all in the direction of higher performance in the nonstandardized as compared with the standardized condition, the second testing (T2) as compared with the first testing (T1), and of course on the high—low performance on the blocked variables. For Matrices, a significant interaction was detected between condition and time, with the highest performance on the nonstandardized condition at time 2. For Order of Appearance, a trend in this direction was found, but it was not significant ($F = 2.47$, df = 1 / 44, $p = .12$). No interactions between either condition or testing time and the blocked variables were found, indicating homogeneity of regression and no statistically significant differential relationships between the manipulations and the achievement variables.

DISCUSSION / The main expectation of this investigation that mode of test administration and simple test repetition can lead to higher levels of performance was supported. Since the majority of evidence on the effects of training on the acquisition of concrete operational thought structures suggests that training is effective for children at the transitional stage only, children whose cognitive structures are in the process of consolidation, it appears as though activation or elaboration was involved rather than acquisition of totally new structures. The significant improvement of test results through test repetition regardless of condition lends support to this conclusion as it does not seem plausible that mere test repetition in the standard condition in which the child was not informed in any way concerning his performance could lead to the development of cognitive structures that were not there in some form in the first place. Thus, the results are in agreement with a point made by Overton, Wagner and Dolinsky (1971) that the transitional period is one in which present but not fully consolidated structures may be activated by various task manipulations and lead to higher levels of performance; performance which is more indicative of the child's actual level of development or competence than would be assessed by standard procedures.

Another aspect involved is the accurate assessment of level of cognitive development for children with fully formed structures. Performance levels below actual capability stem from several sources as outlined by Smedslund (1969). But regardless of this, if levels of the child's performance, whether he is in a transitional phase of development or already at the level of concrete operational thought, are below what he is capable of, Type II error or concluding false negatives is involved. In the 'testing-the-limits' approach where the attempt to gain maximum performance is employed as it was in this investigation, simple, standardized procedures are reliable, but may fall short on assessing what the child can actually do.

Inspection of the correlations (see Table 4) of the Matrices and Order of Appearance tests with the various measures of achievement reveal that the correlations of both Piaget measures with teachers' judgments of achievement and potential tend to be lowest for the standard condition, time 1 testing. In fact for both Matrices and Order of Appearance the correlations obtained in the standard condition at time 1 were not significantly different from zero. For the nonstandard condition group tested at time 2 (standard conditions), however, all correlations were significant with values of around .50. The correlations with the Piaget tests and the standardized achievement test scores (math and reading) do not tend to vary in the different conditions or times of testing. They remain low. This result was expected inasmuch as standardized achievement tests are performance tests that may or may not accurately assess a child's maximum potential. The Q-sorts resulting from teachers' judgments of potential and achievement, on the other hand, were expected to be more accurate measures of the child's competence as the teachers knew the children very well as they had worked with them for the entire school year in self-contained classrooms.

In order to test for the differential relationships between the most efficient predictor variables, as determined by regression analysis, and the Piaget tests, analysis of variance procedures were employed with high—low blocking on the most salient predictors. These were teachers' judgment of reading achievement for Matrices and teachers' judgment of math potential for Order of Appearance. The nonsignificant

interactions between these variables and condition or time for both
Matrices and Order of Appearance indicated that the slopes of the
regression lines were parallel. Thus, although correlations tend to
increase between the Piaget measures in the nonstandard condition and
at time 2 over the standard condition at time 1 with teacher judgments
of achievement and potential, the magnitude of this increase is not
statistically significant.

*Task structure and transfer in children's learning of double
classification skills*
J.L. Caruso and L.B. Resnick, 1972

AIM / The study attempted verification of a task analysis and the
hypothesized hierarchy of double classification tasks.

SUBJECTS / N = 26, with CA five years six months and were
predominantly black. None of the subjects was initially capable of
solving the double classification problems.

METHOD / Subjects were trained on three different matrix tasks in
either the optimal (simplest to most complex) or reverse sequence. Two
training groups were therefore established. The tests used were
variations of the matrix task often employed in studies of double
classification with children (Inhelder and Piaget, 1964).
The requirement of the tasks used in training was to select, from an
array of objects, the one which correctly filled each empty cell of the
matrix. 'Each task involved a different type of empty cell,
corresponding to the cells labeled one, two and three . . . The proposed
hierarchy of three double classification tasks was derived from a
behaviour analysis which suggested major differences in the operations
involved, depending on the pattern of empty and filled cells . . . In
order to solve cell type one (ie an empty cell to whose row and column
each have two already filled cells), the child would have to be able to
perform (certain, word inserted) behaviours . . . For cell type two (ie
two filled cells in one direction — row or column — but only one in the
other direction), the solution process is more complex, because the
child cannot directly name a common row (or column) attribute.
Therefore, he must answer "no" to the question in Box A . . . Cell three
is still more difficult to solve because neither attribute can be directly
determined from objects already in the row or column . . . it was
hypothesized that tasks involving empty cells of the three
types . . . would form a learning hierarchy, with cells of type one at the
simplest level, cells of type three at the most complex level, and cells of

type two intermediate', pp. 1298–1299.

The training tasks were administered twice to the subjects: in a pre-test form and under training conditions. No training was given on the transfer task — this was also presented twice: in the pre-test and after the training phase as a post-test. (Fuller details of the pretraining task, the three training tasks and the transfer task are described in Caruso and Resnick, 1972, pp. 1302–1304.)

RESULTS / The authors conclude, 'More optimal sequence subjects learned the tasks, and they learned in fewer trials than did reverse sequence subjects. These subjects, together with the pass—fail patterns among the tasks, confirm the hypothesized relationship. They also suggest the power of hierarchically sequenced training in the acquisition of specific cognitive skills. Positive transfer to an untrained matrix task with similar task structure lends further support to the task analysis on which the hierarchical predictions were based', p. 1297.

Assessment and training of role-taking and referential communication skills in institutionalized emotionally disturbed children
M.J. Chandler, S. Greenspan, and C. Barenboim, 1974

AIM / The authors formulated three hypotheses as follows: (a) That institutionalized emotionally disturbed children, characterized by chronic social adjustment problems, would evidence pronounced developmental delays in the development of role-taking and referential communication skills; (b) that such development deficits would be partially remediated through programmes of communication and role-taking training; (c) that such changes would be accompanied by measurable improvements in social competence.

SUBJECTS / Different numbers of Ss participated in different phases of the research design. Screening or pre-test phase involved an assessment of the social role-taking and referential communication skills of 125 emotionally disturbed children between the ages of eight and 15. On the basis of the screening test, 48 Ss (CA from nine to 14 years) were selected who, relative to both their normal age-mates and their institutionalized peers, evidenced marked delays in the acquisition of both referential and role taking skills. The 48 Ss were then assigned to three treatment conditions — 16 in each of the two training phases and the remaining 16 were placed in a non-treatment control group.

METHOD / The test of role-taking ability was patterned after Flavell *et al.* (1968) and further elaborated by Chandler (1971, 1972, 1973).

The measure of referential communication skills used followed that
described by Greenspan and Chandler (1973) which incorporated
features previously developed by Botkin (1966), Glucksberg, Krauss,
and Weisberg (1966), Cowan (1966), and Shantz and Wilson (1972).
Following the initial assessment phase, the 48 Ss who had performed at
the lower levels of the screening tests were randomly assigned to one of
the three treatment conditions. One third of the Ss were placed in a
non treatment control group. In the role-taking training, 'Following an
intervention strategy developed and tested with groups of highly
egocentric delinquent boys (Chandler, 1973), 16 Ss were enrolled in an
experimental training programme that employed drama and the making
of video films as vehicles for providing remedial training in deficient
role-taking skills', p. 549. Referential communication training was given
to another 16 Ss. The procedures were patterned after training phases
of Botkin (1966) and Shantz and Wilson (1972) and were similar to the
conservation training procedures of Inhelder and Sinclair (1969),
Smedslund (1968) and Siegel, Roeper, and Hooper (1968) in that an
effort was made to bring about a state of 'cognitive conflict' or
disequilibrium through the use of feedback regarding inadequacies in
communication performance. These procedures are fully described in
Greenspan, Zlotlow, Burka, and Barenboim (1973).

RESULTS / The institutionalized Ss were found to be delayed
significantly in the acquisition of both role-taking and referential
communication when compared with samples of their normal
age-mates. Pre- and post-intervention comparisons demonstrated that Ss
of both experimental groups enhanced significantly in their role-taking
ability. Ss of the communication training programme likewise indicated
significant improvement in referential communication skills. A
12-month follow-up indicated a trend for improvements in both test
measures to be associated with improvements in social adjustment.

*Amenability to incorrect hypotheses in the extinction of conservation
of weight in college students*
M.J. Chiseri, 1975

AIM / To test the hypothesis that the conservation questionnaire
would render college students more amenable to an unexpected
instance of non-conservation of weight, and thus less likely to resist
extinction.

SUBJECTS / N = 54 university psychology students.

METHOD / 'Prior to the extinction trial each S was given a three-page booklet and asked to complete the task on the first page and not to work ahead. The postulated amenability to extinction was induced in half the group by written instructions to fill in the conservation questionnaire as follows: Conservation is a term used to describe the situation when an attribute or property (e.g., weight) of an object remains unchanged through certain changes in other attributes of that object. The table . . . refers to certain changes that might be applied to an object and the respective effects on two quantitative properties, weight and mass. Your task is to fill in the table. Decide whether the property "always", "sometimes", or "never" conserves under each of the given changes. The control half of the sample was instructed to "free associate" to each of 15 stimulus words appearing on the first page of their booklet and to write down their spontaneous impressions to such terms as "flower", "sky", "school". This task was interpreted as not relevant to conservation and tantamount to a neutral set regarding conservation and extinction . . . Next, two balls of green modelling clay were placed on a . . . scale and shown to be of equal weight. The E then took one of the balls and . . . flattened it into a hamburger shape. While compressing the clay a tiny lead weight was surreptitiously inserted into it. The students were asked to predict whether the unaltered ball and hamburger would weigh the same. After writing down their predictions, they were shown that the hamburger weighed more than the ball . . . the Ss were directed to turn the page and perform the designated task. The Ss who did the conservation questionnaire prior to the extinction trial now did the free association . . . ' p. 121.

RESULTS / That the adult Ss were 'primed to "extinguish" and it is therefore less than surprising that the large majority in Hall and Kingsley's study failed to attend to some form of the simple addition—subtraction rationale. To judge from Miller *et al.*, Hall and Kingsley and the present study, it appears that adults, if allowed sufficient latitude and not intimidated by technicalities of content, will sustain a conservation hypothesis in extinction paradigms,' p. 142.

*The young child's representation of another's view**
M.V. Cox, 1976

In this study, the developmental changes which occur as the child

---

* Written and prepared by the author for inclusion in this volume.
Gratitude is extended to Dr Maureen Cox of the University of York

learns to represent another person's view (perspective ability) were examined. Efforts to devise an unambiguous task for investigating these changes suggested that task variables affect the child's performance: 1. Six-year-olds who predicted the experimenter's view found the task easier than those who predicted their own view from another position or a doll's view (experiment 1). 2. Children found the task easier when illustrations represented the views than when models were used (experiment 2). 3. Children found the view from opposite them more difficult to predict than views from side positions (experiment 4).

It was found that in the development of perspective ability, the representation of before—behind relationships normally precedes that of left—right relationships when both are presented together; this order applied to all the different object arrangements and observed positions (experiments 4 and 5). When the relationships were presented separately, however, this order was less clear: by the age of seven the children appeared equally competent in representing before—behind and left—right relationships (experiment 3). There was evidence that the earliest step in the representation of another's view may be the correct location of the object nearest to the other observer (experiment 4); this may, however, be specific to certain object arrangements (experiment 5).

In order to produce conditions conducive to the study of the causes of transition from stage to stage, a training programme which accelerated the normal development of perspective ability was employed (experiment 6). Three feedback methods of training were compared in experiment 7. Although children who moved to the other observer's position to check their responses improved their performance compared with controls, they did not sustain this superiority or transfer their learning to other tasks; training which provided feedback (visual or verbal) about another's view while the child was confronted by his own view proved more successful.

The effects of drill on addition—subtraction fact learning; with implication of Piagetian reversibility
T.E. Davidson, 1975

AIM / To investigate the relationship between addition and subtraction as inverse operations, 'to determine how drill in addition facts will affect knowledge of subtraction facts; to infer, if possible, when addition is conceptualized as an operation with reversibility; and to determine at which grade levels a particular method of drill is effective'.

SUBJECTS / N = 1007 from elementary and secondary grades.

METHOD / The treatment comprised of administering drill on the addition facts, to classroom groups using the overhead projector. Two tests were administered three times, at the beginning of the study, after one week and after two weeks. The Addition Facts Test contained 100 basic addition facts and the Subtraction Facts Test 100 basic subtraction facts. 'Four scores were considered for each test; "time", the "number left out", the "number missed", and the "total error". Gain scores showing loss or progress from the pre-test to each of the two post-tests were computed for each of these four scores', p. 102—A.

RESULTS / The data was subjected to correlation coefficients and two-way analyses of variance. 'On nine scores there were large differences between first and second grade groups. The results are consistent with what one would expect if first grade students had not formed the concept of addition as an operation with reversibility. The results are consistent with what one would expect if: at the second grade level, addition were conceptualized as an operation with reversibility for a good portion of the students, yet there were a good number for whom this reversibility were limited or inoperative; the concept of addition as an operation continued to develop with a more pronounced reversibility during grades three and four', (*ibid.*, p. 102—A).

Cognitive style and reasoning about speed
L.C. Ehri and I.M. Muzio, 1974

The authors maintain that Pascual-Leone (1970) has suggested that 'Piaget's theory of intellectual functioning be extended to include a central processor or computing space whose function it is to transform and coordinate information and whose capacity expands as the child grows . . . reported evidence indicating that field dependent subjects, unlike field independent subjects, often fail to utilize the full structural capacities of their central processors . . . As a consequence, these Ss display reasoning patterns similar to those of younger children observed by Piaget and Inhelder (1941)', p. 569.

AIM / The authors were intent to establish whether alternative solutions to the problem of moving merry-go-round might be related to differences in field dependency.

SUBJECTS / N = 61. Ss were students enrolled at the University of

California.

METHOD / Field dependence was measured with an embedded figures test, the Components subtest (Flanagan Aptitude Classification Test, 1958).

The four merry-go-round problems were stated verbally. 'The first instructed Ss to think of a merry-go-round which has two circles of horses. One circle is on the outside of the platform. The other circle is on the inside. Billy selects a horse on the outside to ride. Danny picks a horse in the inside. The merry-go-round begins turning. Is one boy going faster than the other boy or are they both going the same speed? The Ss were required to check one of the three alternatives (i.e. outside faster, inside faster, same speed) and then to explain their choice. Three problems . . . required Ss to notice differences in distance travelled by tracing the routes of the horses, to think about an analogous situation in which children hold hands and run around a post . . . and to consider the formula for speed . . . ', p. 570.

RESULTS / The reasoning demonstrated by the subjects supported Pascual-Leone's (1970) information processing model. ' . . . unlike field independent subjects who reasoned correctly from the outset, field dependent subjects failed to think analytically. They were misled by perceptually salient aspects of the situation; they tended to center on these features in their reasoning; and they resisted accommodating to additional information', p. 569.

*The acquisition of Piagetian conservation by children in school — a training programme**
L.G. Ellis, 1972

AIM / It was postulated that the cognitive strategy which effectuates conservation is the result of the fusion of a number of crucial mental operations and that the sequential acquisition of these prerequisites would construct the cognitive structure necessary for conservation to be discovered as a principle. As the aim was to train the underlying 'mother structure', gains would occur across the horizontal *décalage*. Training was to be undertaken by class teachers under classroom conditions and it was to derive from conflict / equilibration theory, 'feedback' being eliminated. Additionally, the training was to be designed to compare the relative efficacy of 'Free' and 'Structured'

*   Written and prepared by the author for inclusion in this volume. Gratitude is
    extended to Lew G. Ellis of the University of Leicester.

teaching methods.

The stability of the gains was to be examined by subjecting them to contrasuggestion designed to extinguish — the durable residue of gains being the index of support for the hypothesis, if any.

SAMPLE / The population (105) of the infant department of Hampshire primary J and I school from which 28 'trios' were selected matched on the criteria of:

(i) A thirteen item conservation (pre) test battery of Number, Continuous Quantity, Discontinuous Quantity, Mass, Weight, Length after repositioning, Length after partioning, Area — smaller from larger congruent, Area after subdivision, Complementary Area, Interior Volume, Occupied Volume and Displaced Volume. Each test consisted of three stages which progressively exaggerated the perceptual cues towards non-conservation. Each stage was questioned and both the testees' responses and their reasons for giving them were scored.
(ii) Scores on the Board form of Raven's Coloured Matrices and the Crichton Vocabulary Scale.
(iii) Sex
(iv) Age

Control was maintained by the 'double blind' procedure.

The sample was divided into three Age Groups (A, B and C) with age ranges of 7.1 — 6.4 years (Mean 6.7), 6.3 — 5.6 years (Mean 5.10) and 5.5 — 5.0 years (Mean 5.3) respectively.

The members of the matched trios within each Age Group were then randomly assigned to one of three Treatment Groups — 'Structured', 'Free' or 'Control' — as under:

Age Gp.	Treatment Groups			Trainer
'A'	'a' (Structured)	'b' (Free)	'c' (Control)	Cl. Tch. 'X'
N = 30	N = 10	N = 10	N = 10	
'B'				
N = 27	'a' N = 9	'b' N = 9	'c' N = 9	Cl. Tch. 'Y'
'C'				
N = 27	'a' N = 9	'b' N = 9	'c'N = 9	Cl. Tch. 'Z'

METHOD / Many previous researchers — e.g. Lovell and Ogilvie (1960), Wohlwill and Lowe (1962), Zimiles (1963), Wallach and Sprott (1964), Frank (1964), Wallach, Wall and Anderson (1967), Sigel, Roeper and Hooper (1966), Halford and Fullerton (1970), Halford (1970) — conclude that conservation fails to be attained because of what Bruner, Olver and Greenfield (1966) so aptly call 'perceptual seduction'. Halford (1970) goes so far as to say that the conservation of number is acquired when the recognition of the compensating relationships which exists between dimensions renders the perceptual cues 'acceptable'. Yet, as Wallach (1969) points out, the exactly compensating nature of the changing dimensions on deformation of a stimulus array is so fantastically complicated as to defy recognition in all but the simplest of cases. For this reason this possible route to conservation has been ignored by researchers.

The only conceivable 'carrier' of this information *per se* is atomism. With this in mind, a series of wooden blocks was constructed, the individual members of which could be related to other members on the criteria of any, or all, of their dimensions and masses. In addition, all the blocks could be replicated by assembling numbers of the smallest (unit) block in a variety of ways, i.e.:

Cross sections of blocks

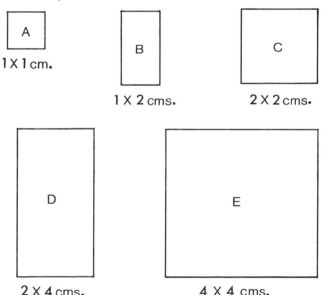

A
1 X 1 cm.

B
1 X 2 cms.

C
2 X 2 cms.

D
2 X 4 cms.

E
4 X 4 cms.

Lengths of blocks — 1 @ 6cms (A), 1 @ 12 cms (B), 1 @ 18 cms (C) and 1 @ 24 cms (D) of each cross section — a total of 20 blocks.

Relationships between blocks —
   2 x Aa = Ab and Ba
   2 x Ab = Ac, Bb, Da
     Ad = 2 x Ac, Bc, Db etc.

Cognition of the exact reciprocity of changing dimensions is, however, only the culminating notion of a sequence leading to conservation.

Zimiles (1963) suggests that early perceptions are based exclusively on cues of Length, Height, Width, Density etc. and so constitute the definition, in so far as there is a definition, of quantity, for the non-conserving child. Lovell and Ogilvie (1960), among others, concluded that non-conservers failed because of 'centering on one dimension', while Sigel, Roeper and Hooper (1966) achieved some success by inducing their Ss to respond to multi-dimensional objects. Piaget (1952b) suggests that, in order to conserve, a child must first be able to perform operations of multiple classification, and multiplicative relationality.

The route towards conservation starts at the point where the child ceases to base his judgments of 'same' and 'different' on the evidence of an object's single attribute. He proceeds when he perceives that objects can be classified and reclassified, and hence related and re-related, on any, or all, of their discrete attributes. He makes a major step forward when he accepts that compared objects can be 'the same' and 'different' simultaneously.

Eight training sessions were designed to offer children experiences of Classification and Multiple Classification, Relationality and Multiplicative Relationality. Operations of Atomism were incorporated via which the cognition of the reciprocity of the dimensions of equal masses might be acquired. A ninth session of thirty minutes' duration, as were the others, offered training in Reversibility with the aim of consolidating the crystalising cognitive structure.

A set of twelve similar dolls, each having six discrete attributes (sex, hair colour, articles of clothing) on the evidence of which they might be classified with, and related to, other dolls, was used for the first three training sessions.

In all but the last of the remaining sessions the blocks described above were used to transmit first notions of multiple classification and multiplicative relationality on the criteria of their masses and dimensions and finally, via atomism, cognition of the exact reciprocity of the dimensions of similar masses.

There was little danger of 'test reinforcement' as the training apparatus differed greatly from that used in the testing. In addition, 'feedback' was eliminated from the training, the children being led into conflict situations, the resolution of which would effect the necessary internal restructuring.

The 'structured treatment groups' of each age group were led through the predetermined programme as a group. With the 'Free Groups' attempts were made to tailor the programme to the needs of individual children. Each child received personal and individual treatment and this, of necessity, meant that he would engage in free play with the apparatus, or work on assignments left by the trainer, when she was engaged with other group members.

The training timetable was so arranged as to give all groups equal shares of high and low 'attention span' time and provision was made against the Hawthorne effect with the control groups.

Finally, extinction procedures, incorporating contrasuggestion, were used to assess the quality of the natural gains made by the control groups during the training period and the trained gains of those children who had received treatment.

RESULTS / The formula

$$ t = \frac{Md}{\sqrt{\dfrac{\dfrac{\Sigma d^2}{N} - Md^2}{N-1}}} $$

was used to determine:
1. Any significant differences between treatment groups on initial matching.
2. Any significant differences between gains after training
   a. Within each age group.
   b, Within the sample.
   c. Across the *horizontal décalage*.
   d. After the application of extinction procedures.

It was found that:
1. All but one of the trained groups had made significantly greater gains than had the control groups.
2. All the 'Structured' groups had made greater gains than had the 'Free' groups. When these comparisons were made within the total sample, the difference reached statistical significance.

In all cases the results given are for one-tailed tests.

3. The trained gains had generalised across the *horizontal décalage*, though not uniformly — (see over)

4. Extinction procedures produced greater losses with the trained than

Treatment groups compared

	Structured and control	Free and control	Structured and free
Age group 'A' df = 9	t = 2.755 P < 0.025 St > c	t = 2.412 P < 0.025 Fr > c	t = 0.736 P > 0.100 St > Fr
Age group 'B' df = 8	t = 2.771 P < 0.025 St > c	t = 1.684 P < 0.100 Fr > c	t = 1.527 P < 0.100 St > Fr
Age group 'C' df = 8	t = 2.694 P < 0.025 St > c	t = 2.805 P < 0.025 Fr > c	t = 1.002 P > 0.100 St > Fr
Total sample df = 27	t = 4.889 P < 0.0005 St > c	t = 3.642 P < 0.005 Fr > c	t = 1.801 P < 0.050 St > Fr

with the control groups, but the differences were only marginal and did not reach statistical significance —

	Treatment groups compared	
	Structured and control	*Free and control*
Total sample	t = 0.885 P > 0.100	t = 0.346 P > 0.100

Nor did the extinction procedures, applied to those Ss who had achieved full conservation in any test, produce a significant decrement with any group other than the combined Free group.

Structured Gp.	t = 0.556: df = 15: P > 0.100
Free Gp.	t = 1.988: df = 12: P < 0.050
Control Group	t = 0.063: df = 6: P > 0.100

5. The greatest gains were made by the most backward children

e.g. Helen, aged 6.2. Pre-Test Cons. Score 2, Post-Test 36 / 78
David, aged 6.1. Pre-Test Cons. Score 0, Post-Test 53 / 78
Richard, aged 5.2. Pre-Test Cons. Score 3, Post-Test 35 / 78

All three were members of trained groups and all had Ravens / Crichton Scores below the 10th Percentile.

Treatment groups compared (total sample) df = 27

Test		Structured and control		Free and control
1.	Number	t = 4.825 P < 0.0005	St > c	t = 4.482 P < 0.0005	Fr > c
2.	Continuous Quantity	t = 3.199 P < 0.005	St > c	t = 4.106 P < 0.0005	Fr > c
3.	Discontinuous Quantity	t = 2.110 P < 0.025	St > c	t = 2.269 P < 0.025	Fr > c
4.	Mass	t = 5.102 P < 0.0005	St > c	t = 3.032 P < 0.005	Fr > c
5.	Weight	t = 2.661 P < 0.010	St > c	t = 2.546 P < 0.010	Fr > c
6.	Length re- positioned	t = 2.355 P < 0.025	St > c	t = 1.781 P < 0.050	Fr > c
7.	Length partitioned	t = 3.536 P < 0.005	St > c	t = 2.815 P < 0.005	Fr > c
8.	Area sub- tracted	t = 1.477 P < 0.100	St > c	t = 0.316 P > 0.100	Fr > c
9.	Area partitioned	t = 3.690 P < 0.0005	St > c	t = 2.241 P < 0.025	Fr > c
10.	Area Complementary	t = 3.738 P < 0.0005	St > c	t = 1.752 P < 0.050	Fr > c
11.	Volume – Interior	t = 2.782 P < 0.005	St > c	t = 1.697 P < 0.100	Fr > c
12.	Volume – Occupied	t = 1.441 P < 0.100	St > c	t = 0.109 P > 0.100	Fr > c
13.	Volume – Displaced	t = 0.593 P > 0.100	St > c	t = 1.087 P > 0.100	Fr > c

CONCLUSIONS /

1. Conservation can be discovered as a principle via a logical sequence of experiences designed to develop a strategy for the handling of perceptual cues.

2. Conservation is acquired when the exact reciprocity of relationships after deformation is understood and the carrier of this information is atomism. There are possibly other ways of arriving at conservation.

3. The strategy, once learned, generalises in varying degrees across the *horizontal décalage*. Other factors might well impede its application in some conservation situations — further research along these lines would prove interesting and probably profitable.

4. Conflict / equilibration methods of training are effective and produce durable learning which resists extinction.

5. 'Free' methods, as defined in this work, were less effective than the structured training in this study. The reasons for this were:

   (a) The sequence of experiences, as defined in the training programme, was less closely followed with the Free groups than with the structured groups.

   (b) The time available for training was less profitably used by the free groups than by the structured groups. In the latter case no time was spent on 'undirected activities' while, with the free groups, 42% of the training time was spent by children engaging themselves in activities having no possible connection with the training. Time spent on free play with the apparatus is not included in that figure because of its probable training value.

6. Backward children are well able to build the cognitive structure of conservation and to use the then available strategy. This probably has far reaching implications as to the nature of their specific deprivation and for the cultural deprivation hypothesis in general. Further research could well lead to effective compensation techniques.

7. Future training attempts based on conceptual analysis may well lead to effective teaching methods. As 'intelligence' might be defined as 'problem solving ability' and is possibly a complex arrangement of cognitive strategies, the field is large.

Long-term effects of conservation training with educationally subnormal children
D. Field, 1974

AIM / To discover the variables which were critical to the development of Piagetian conservation in ESN children by replicating and comparing the Learning Set method (Gelman, 1969) and the Verbal Rule method (Beilin, 1965).

Experiment One

SUBJECTS / N = 56 ESN children were pre-tested: 12 of these were 'natural' conservers, and seven conserved number only; 15 were eliminated because their MA was below four years 11 months. The remaining 22 children were ranked by MA and assigned to one of the three experimental groups.

METHOD / The pre-test proceeded in the unvarying order of number, mass, length and weight. The Peabody Picture Vocabulary Test (Dunn, 1965) was used to help the Ss being assigned to one of the three groups, 'so any subsequent differences between the groups cannot be attributed to differences in verbal abilities', p. 238. Each S participated in three individual training sessions: Learning Set (Gelman, 1969); Verbal Rule (Beilin, 1965); and Control group in which the Ss also had three individual sessions: E and S played the game of Draughts. The post-test similar to the pre-test was administered four to five days after the third training.

Experiment Two

POST-TEST TWO / After one year four months 21 of the Ss were given post-test two which was identical to post-test one.

METHOD / The PPVT, Form B, was given and one training session was administered. For every child, the type of retraining was identical as the original training of experiment one. Five to 10 days after 'the one-shot retraining', post-test three was given, identical to post-tests one and two.

Experiment Three

The results of experiments one and two supported the conclusion that the Verbal Rule method was an effective way to inculcate conservation skills in educationally subnormal children and 'that this method was the cause of the observed changes of behaviour. To dispel any question, however, two months after Experiment Two was concluded, the Ss from Group L and Group C who were not yet conservers were formed into a new group, Group R. Eleven Ss remained to form Group R: four from Group C and seven from Group L', p. 242.

METHOD / Subjects in Group R were trained by the Verbal Rule method as in experiment one. The training sessions took the same number of days. The post-test four was identical to those which had preceded it.

RESULTS / After the first post-test the Verbal Rule method proved superior to the Learning Set method. The author argued that this may be a qualitative difference between normal and subnormal children, 'but there is no doubt in this study that the long-lasting results were produced by the Verbal Rule method. It is important to note that the justification answers given by the Verbal Rule — trained Ss in both training experiments included the concepts of identity, reversibility, and compensation', p. 244. However, Bovet, Sinclair and Smock (1966) were not able to demonstrate this and concluded that it was not possible to induce such complete understanding.

The effects of training in conservation of tonal and rhythmic patterns on second-grade children
E.A. Foley, 1975

AIM / To examine the effects of training on the conservation of tonal patterns under the 'deformation' of rhythmic patterns and the conservation of rhythmic patterns under the 'deformation' of tonal patterns.

SUBJECTS / Children were drawn from six second grade classes.

METHOD / Ss in three of the classes received the training programme while the Ss in the remaining three classes served as the control group. 'The specific training programme devised for use in the study was based on procedures previously found to be effective in improving conservation ability either in music or in other fields of study . . . the conservation test was administered as a pre-test to one-half of the Ss in each of the six classes.' After the training the conservation test was given as a post-test to the remaining Ss in each class. A delayed post-test, two weeks after the initial post-test, was administered to all Ss who had taken the initial post-test. 'This was done in order to determine whether any improvement in conservation ability which might have occurred during the training period could be retained over a period of time.'

RESULTS / The experimental group demonstrated a significant (.01 level) increase in conservation scores, while the control group's increase was not significant. There was no significant difference in scores among the three control classes or among the three experimental classes. Neither the control group nor the experimental group indicated a significant decrease in scores from the initial post-test to the delayed post-test. Overall, the results demonstrated that training enhanced conservation performance of tonal and rhythmic patterns.

Hypothesis sampling systems among preoperational and concrete operational kindergarten children
B. Gholson, J. O'Connor and I. Stern, 1976

AIM / To test some implications of Piagetian theory in a conventional discrimination-learning task.

SUBJECTS / N = 452 middle class kindergarten children. Following a pre-test each of 60 concrete operational and pre-operational children participated in the study. The remaining 323 were eliminated because they were transitional (Beilin, 1971; Piaget, 1952b). The 120 Ss were assigned to treatment conditions as follows: 30 concrete operational Ss to an experimental group (mean CA = 5:7); 30 pre-operational Ss to an experimental group (mean CA = 5:5); 30 concrete operational Ss to a control group (mean CA = 5:7) and 30 pre-operational Ss to a control group (mean CA = 5:7).

METHOD / Conservation pre-test: Each S was individually tested on the number and liquid quantity conservation tasks to diagnose cognitive status (Beilin, 1969; Flavell, 1963; Gelman, 1969; Piaget, 1952b; and Siegler and Liebert, 1972).

Stimulus Differentiation Training: Half the Ss of each developmental level were alternately assigned to an experimental and half to a control condition. All children solved 24 stimulus differentiation problems each six trials in length during this phase of training. These were patterned after Gholson and McConville (1974).

Discrimination Learning: Each S was presented with a series of four-dimensional simultaneous discrimination-learning problems. The same four dimensions (alphabetic letter, size, colour, line position) were used in each problem, but each used a different pair of 10 letters and six colours.

In sum each S received stimulus differentiation training either with feedback (experimental groups) or without (control groups), prior to a series of discrimination-learning problems in which a blank-trial probe, employed to detect the child's hypothesis, followed each feedback trial. (Fuller details of the experimental procedure are given in Gholson, O'Connor and Stern, 1976, pp. 65—68.)

RESULTS / The authors conclude, 'The results of the present study appear to provide strong support for the Piagetian view that (some) cognitive capacities are stage dependent with information processing efficiency contingent upon developmental level. While the four groups of the main experiment did not differ in chronological age (nor did the groups of transitional children), the concrete operational children manifested significantly superior performances on all but one of the eight dependent measures examined ($p < .10$ in that case). There were also, however, significant effects of feedback condition upon three dependent measures. Children of both cognitive levels who received feedback during stimulus differentiation training were more likely to abandon a disconfirmed hypothesis and to resample locally consistent hypotheses than were the controls. Further, the concrete operational subjects manifested significantly more strategy systems under the experimental than the control condition (75 vs. 45 per cent . . .). These results, along with others, suggest that the Piagetian view does not tell the whole story . . . ', (*ibid.*, pp. 73–74).

Negative effects of the pre-test in training conservation of length
G. Greitzer and W.E. Jeffrey, 1973

AIM / The authors maintain that previous training studies have proved generally unsuccessful 'due to inadequate control for negative transfer effects of the pre-test'. Such a possibility in training length conservation was investigated.

SUBJECTS / N = 44, with an age-range of four years and five years two months.

METHOD / 'Two procedures, each consisting of 11 non-reinforced trials, were employed. A fading procedure was developed in which the first trial was a collinear transformation, with subsequent trials successively approximating the standard conservation test. A modified version of Gelman's (1969) learning set training serves as an alternative procedure. One half of the subjects were pre-tested, the other half were not. Thus, the training procedures and the pre-test–no-pre-test conditions formed a 2 x 2 factorial design. In addition, a control group of 11 subjects received pre- and post-testing but no training. The pre-test consisted of one conservation test involving a horizontal transformation and occurred on average 10.6 days prior to training and / or the post-test (training and the post-test were given in the same session). Subjects who conserved on the pre-test (9 per cent) were retained in the experiment as a control for the performance of natural conservers in the non-pre-tested groups', p. 435.

RESULTS / The effect of the pre-test on the number of trials correct in training was significant. Learning set training was superior to fading training. Negative transfer effects from the pre-test to post-test were indicated for both types of training. 'The pre-test may increase the salience of misleading cues, in particular, that of the transformation itself. The absence of this cue in learning set training leads to correct responding, but its reappearance in the post-test produces non-conservation. Pre-tested fading training fails due to the transformation cue on the collinear trial. Without a pre-test, however, both procedures establish length as the appropriate cue', p. 435.

Acquisition of conservation through learning a consistent classificatory system for quantities
G.S. Halford, 1971

AIM / Following Piaget's (1950) assertion that logic is the mirror of thought, the study attempted to induce acquisition of conservation of quantity employing the principle that 'conservation results from attempts to build a consistent representation of quantities in thought'.

SUBJECTS / Thirty two subjects were non-conservers on the test patterned after Halford (1968). 'The 32 Ss were randomly selected from 60 subjects who failed the conservation test. The 16 conservation (C) subjects were randomly selected from 60 subjects who passed the conservation test. Sixteen of the non-conservation (N) subjects were allocated to the experimental or training (T) group, and 16 to the control or waiting (W) group at random', p. 154. Mean age of C group was 77.9 months – mean age of T group was 70.30 months, and mean age of W was 71.6 months.

METHOD / Twelve problems were involved, and subject and experimenter each had a set of containers for each problem. Different sets of containers were employed for each problem. The designations of the specific containers were patterned after Halford (1968, 1969) and the material used was rice.

The general plan of the experiment was as follows: 'After the conservation of quantity pre-tests the training group (T) subjects were given learning set training . . . During this period the control or waiting (W) subjects and the conservation (C) subjects were not tested at all. When learning set training was complete, all groups were given a further conservation test, using one of the sets of containers . . . under "substitution procedure". Then all groups were given training designed to teach them that when two sets of material are initially equal, they

may be substituted for one another in a common measure, irrespective of any changes of shape one of them may undergo. Having witnessed this demonstration, the subjects were asked whether the two quantities were still equal. This substitution was both a superficial kind of training in the "fact" of conservation, and a test for understanding of conservation. As a training procedure it contrasts with the learning set procedure which is designed to provide a logical basis for the conservation concept. Following substitution training subjects who had given a conservation response up to this time were given an extinction test by means of a faked demonstration of non-conservation', p. 154.
(Fuller details of the training, the substitution and the extinction procedures are described in Halford, 1971, pp. 155–156).

RESULTS / Fourteen out of 16 subjects in the training group were fully operational, in contrast to only four out of 16 in the control group. 'Then all subjects were given training designed to convince them that two initially equal quantities may still be substituted for one another in a common measure even if they no longer appear to be equal. Finally all conservers were given a faked demonstration of non-conservation. The subjects who had been trained to conserve did not resist this demonstration, whereas 50 per cent of a group of natural conservers did so. The training procedure is discussed in relation to learning and equilibration theory', p. 151.

Identity, reversibility, verbal rule instruction, and conservation
B.R. Hamel and B.O.M. Riksen, 1973

The authors cite the work of Beilin (1965); Gruen (1965); Bruner, Olver and Greenfield (1966); Hamel (1971); and Hamel, Van der Veer and Westerhof (1972) and formulated the following hypotheses.

AIMS / '(a) Subjects given verbal rule instruction identity training perform better than control group subjects on nonspecific transfer conservation tasks. (b) Subjects given verbal rule instruction identity training perform better than those given verbal rule instruction reversibility training on nonspecific transfer conservation tasks. (c) The hypothesized effect in the first hypothesis remains one week after training. (d) The hypothesized effect in the second hypothesis remains one week after training'.

SUBJECTS / N = 60 (mean age five years 10 months). The identity — training group comprised 12 girls and eight boys (non-conservers); the reversibility — training group comprised 14 girls and six boys (non-conservers); and the control group comprised 13 girls and seven boys. A Belgian version of Thurstone's Primary Mental Abilities for ages five to seven (Knops, 1967) was administered to obtain the IQs of the Ss in the various training groups (identity — training group: mean verbal IQ = 116.2; mean perceptual IQ: = 119.7; reversibility — training group: mean verbal IQ: 116.1; mean perceptual IQ: 118.5; Control group: mean verbal IQ = 116.9; mean perceptual IQ: 119.8).

METHOD / *Pre-tests.* These were selected from Form A of the Concept Assessment Kit, (Goldschmid and Bentler, 1968b).

Post-tests. These were selected from Form B of the Concept Assessment Kit, (Goldschmid and Bentler, *op. cit.*)

Training. These included identity and reversibility training sessions. Each subject of the two groups of 20 non-conservers was administered a different kind of verbal rule instruction. The control group of 20 received no training. Fuller details of the pretests, posttests and training sessions are described in Hamel and Riksen, (1973, pp. 67—68).

RESULTS / The data was subjected to Kruskal — Wallis one-way analysis of variance (H) and the Mann — Whitney U test (Siegel, 1956). The resultant patterns demonstrated that both of the training procedures — identity and reversibility — 'resulted in nonspecific transfer to conservation of two-dimensional space, number, substance and weight. A week later these training effects were still evident. The group which has received the verbal rule instruction focused on identity profited significantly more from the training than did the other group. The explanation offered is that the subjects receiving identity training could incorporate the verbal rule given, since it was compatible with their developmental level', p. 66.

Control of the conservation response through discrimination learning set training for conserving and non conserving transformations
B.B. Hamilton, 1973

AIM / The study attempted using discrimination learning set training as a nonverbal method of 'bringing five-year-old children to attend to quantitative dimensions and the behaviour of the E (whether he added or subtracted material or whether he did not) in the conservation task'.

SUBJECTS / N = 80 aged five years.

METHOD / Four experimental groups were formed. These subjects received verbal pretraining in the terms same and different 'through a series of oddity problems before beginning training in (a) oddity only (b) no transformation (NT), (c) conserving transformation (CT), and (d) conserving and non-conserving transformation (CT / NCT). Half of each group further received a repeat question during training in an attempt to inhibit the likelihood of the subject reversing his response when asked twice about the same item. Twenty subjects in each group received post-tests on dimensions used in training (mass and number) and not used in training (length and liquid), post-tests to separate logically responding from instrumentally responding subjects, and post-tests to separate reversing from nonreversing subjects'.

RESULTS / Groups receiving NT, CT, and CT / NCT treatments demonstrated enhanced performances for both specific and nonspecific transfer items. These groups were superior to oddity only (o) 'Repeated questioning procedures were effective in "inoculating" the children against the tendency to reverse answers in the face of a second, identical question. No differences were statistically significant in the separation of logical from instrumental responses'. Results were interpreted as substantiating the contention that 'communication difficulties between the E and child can account for the non-conservation response. Failure to obtain the conserving response is not sufficient evidence for the absence of the Piagetian logical operations. The quality of the conservation response is influenced . . . by the child's attention or inattention to discriminative stimuli in the conservation task. Methodological difficulties in conservation assessment were identified in the child's tendency to reverse himself when asked twice about the same set of stimuli, thus affecting the reliability of the procedure which is generally used to identify non-conserver . . . that discrimination of . . . cues results in increased conservation performance casts doubt on (a) the usefulness of the logical operations as explanatory concepts, (b) the usefulness of conservation tasks as diagnostic tasks, and (c) any assumption made in these tasks as to the exact nature of communication between E and the child'.

Piagetian task performance as a function of training
M.L. Harris, 1974

AIM / The study examined the effectiveness of training prerequisite skills within the context of area conservation, in which subject verbalization was stressed through role-taking on performance of Piagetian tasks.

SUBJECTS / N = 40 non-conserving kindergarten children.

METHOD / Subjects were assigned to control and experimental groups. The latter group was trained to specified criterion levels. Twenty-two criterion tasks were interspersed within the first five training sessions so that the effectiveness of training could be assessed. Pre-test—post-test control group design was employed in a five phase experiment: assessment of prerequisite skills — assessment of possession of conservation concepts by the administration of the Concept Assessment Kit — Conservation (Goldschmid and Bentler, 1968b); individualized training; first post-test to determine effectiveness of training; and two months later the second post-test in order to assess generalizability and durability of training effects.

RESULTS / Training related to the concept of area conservation was successful for subjects ready 'to move into the operational stage of cognitive development . . . the results of this training were found to be durable in that no statistically significant drop in performance levels was detectable two months after cessation of training . . . results of training were found to have generalized in that heightened performance was detected in concept area in which specific training did not take place. The training materials were developed about the basic prerequisite concepts of invariant quantity, reversibility and compensation. Because generalization took place at the same high degree from specific training in area to two-dimensional space, number, substance, continuous quantity, weight, discontinuous quantity, and length, it was inferred that training in any specific area would have been successful if it were built upon the three basic prerequisite concepts . . . The results . . . were more applicable to development of theory than to development of instructional practices . . . The study confirmed the findings of previous research in that reversibility is important as a basic element in training. The study suggests additional research to determine if the role of transformation movement in perceptual change may be equally important as a basic element in training as those of reversibility and compensation'.

Acquisition and retention of classification skills in the trainable mentally retarded
N.K. Klein, 1974

AIM / To induce classification skills in trainable mentally retarded (TMR) children. 'The work of Piaget provided the theoretical framework upon which this study was based'.

SUBJECTS / N = 41 children with an IQ range from 30 to 50 and aged six through twelve years.

METHOD / Subjects were randomly assigned to experimental and control groups. 'A six week intervention was designed for the treatment group to induce classification skills. Each subject received a total of sixty minutes of individualized training, extending over a six week period. The focus of the intervention was on manipulation and exploration of meaningful, concrete materials, leading to the subjects' comprehension of these items in terms of their dimensional attributes of form, size and colour. As soon as these concepts are grasped, subjects were helped to construct groups of like objects of a selected attribute. The intervention included training in classification in single, double and triple schemes, using meaningful familiar toys'. Subjects' responses to concrete and abstract materials were compared by the concrete objects in the Toy Classification Task (TCT) and abstract blocks in the Object Sorting Task (OST). Soon after the intervention the tests administered were termed short term acquisition test (STAT) and those administered seven weeks were referred to as long term retention test (LTRT).

RESULTS / The data were subjected to the analysis of variance technique. 'Test results with the TCT on all schemes (single, double and triple) indicated that the experimental group did show significantly better performance than the control group. There were no significant differences among sorting preferences. There were no significant differences between the performance of the experimental and control group on the OST. Long term retention test results indicated that the experimental group did maintain its advantage over the control group with the meaningful concrete items in the TCT on single, double and triple classification tests. On the OST for LTRT the experimental subjects performed significantly better than controls. There was a high correlation, .70 . . . between the soring scores of the experimental group on concrete and abstract materials in the STAT. This high correlation was not maintained in LTRT'.

A study of the role of manipulatory grouping experience in the classification skill development of young children
R.B. Koon, 1974

AIM / The author was intent to investigate the role of physical experience in the modification of classification skill competence.

SUBJECTS / N = 36 Caucasians within an age range from four to six years.

METHOD / Twelve subjects each were randomly assigned to three experimental conditions — two training and one control group. 'The training consisted of a series of 20 individually conducted, developmentally sequenced, manipulatory grouping experiences with objects through the use of sorting formats, both with and without teacher—child interaction', Piagetian tasks of classificatory ability were administered and were modelled after Kofsky Scalogram of Classificatory Behaviour (Kofsky, 1966). These were used in pre- and post-testing procedures, and the Object Categorization Test, active conditions, (Sigel, Anderson and Shapiro, 1966), used in a post-test only.

RESULTS / The data were subjected to Chi-Square, the Median Test, and the Fisher Exact Probability Test. The results demonstrated that, '1) The group having manipulatory grouping experience with teacher—child interaction, were significantly higher than the control group on pass—fail frequencies made on the classification task series, and no other groups were significantly different; 2) There was no significant difference in the groups on the total number of grouping responses given on the Object Categorization Test; however, the control group used significantly more descriptive responses than the training groups, while both training groups used significantly more relational-contextual and categorical responses than the control group; 3) Sex was not a significant factor in classification skill development; 4) The younger subjects made significantly greater positive change from the pre- to post-test than did the older subjects . . . it was concluded that the manipulatory grouping experience is successful in positively modifying the classification skill competence of young middle class Caucasian children, only in combination with teacher—child inter-action; however, both types of training are successful in inducing greater flexibility of grouping behaviour'.

Mechanisms of change in the development of cognitive structures
D. Kuhn, 1972

AIM / The study was concerned with the mechanisms in terms of which the developmental transformation from one cognitive structure to another occurs. An equilibration model of change (Piaget, 1967) was contrasted with an alternative, imitation model.

SUBJECTS / N = 87 middle class children, from three age groups, four-year-olds, six-year-olds, and eight-year-olds. There were six or seven subjects of each age group in each experimental condition, with two subjects of each age group serving in the control condition.

METHOD / The study made use of the sequence of stages in the child's concepts of classification, Inhelder and Piaget (1964). Six substages in this progression were used, each subject witnessed an adult model sort sets of objects according to one of these stage levels.

'The main set of objects consisted of 12 wooden forms, of four shapes and three colours. Additional sets of items were of varying degrees of similarity to the main set'. (Further details appear in Kuhn, 1972, p. 835.)

The experimental procedure consisted of four phases. In the diagnostic phase each subject was asked to sort collections I, II and III, and was assigned to one of the six stage levels. The modelling phase took place one week later in which an adult model made two sortings at one of the six stage levels, giving reasons for the strategies. The stage at which the model sorted the objects depended on which of four experimental conditions the subject was assigned to. Assignment was counterbalanced with respect to age, sex, pre-test stage level and *décalage* pattern in the pre-test sortings. After the model completed the sortings, the subject was requested to sort all the collections, together with reasons for the sortings. The second post-test took place one week later, consisting of three parts: sortings, 'recall and recognition' and 'preference'. 'Recall and recognition' involved sorting the objects in the way the model had sorted them the previous week and choosing which of several sketches looked most like the model's sorting. 'Preference' involved a response to the request to select the sketch showing the 'best way' of sorting the objects.

RESULTS / The results supported a structural, equilibration model of change in several ways. 'Amount and pattern of change depended on the relation between structural level of model and subject. Children most readily exhibited change in the direction of more-advanced structures. The change that occurred appeared to take place in an invariant sequence of structural transformations.' It was speculated that the observation of a model performing a task in a manner discrepant from (but not inferior to) the child's own conceptualization of the task may be sufficient to induce in the child an awareness of alternative conceptions and will perhaps lead to disequilibrium and reorganization. The essential point appears to be that it is the reorganization of the child's mental operations that constitutes developmental change, and it is only through the exercise of these operations that change occurs.'

*Imitation theory and research from a cognitive perspective**
D. Kuhn, 1973

The author attempted to amend earlier reviews of imitation theory
and research (e.g. Flanders, 1968) in which Piaget's conceptualization
of imitation was omitted.

The author summarized existing theories in two general categories:
those accounting for imitation as a special case of another, more general
form of learning and, accordingly, claim that no special principles are
necessary to account for imitative learning; and those which consider
imitation a unique process or mechanism, which must be accounted for
in its own right. (Kuhn, 1973, pp. 158—61).

Kuhn emphasized that she is describing only a potential theory of
imitation having its basis in Piaget's writings on imitation and in his
general view of cognitive development. From the Piagetian perspective,
imitation is one aspect of the individual's total cognitive functioning.
'In particular, it is the class of (overt or covert) actions characterized by
a "primacy of accommodation over assimilation" (Piaget, 1951).
Adaptation occurs when there is a coordinated and reciprocal
assimilation of external reality to the individual's action schemes and
accommodation of these schemes to reality. Imitation, then, as the
accommodatory pole of cognitive functioning, occurs when there is
accommodation of individual to object without assimilation of the
object to the individual's structure. Thus, imitation is characterized by
an absence of equilibrium between subject and object'.

In Piaget's view imitation does not occur at random: the individual
accommodates to an object or event only insofar as it bears some
relation to his own behavioural structure (Piaget, 1952). Piaget has
traced the origins of imitation through its gradual development during
the sensorimotor period and its consolidation during the preoperational
and concrete operational periods. (Kuhn elaborated this progression,
pp. 161—163). The implications of Piaget's views for a general cognitive
theory are considered by Kuhn to be the assertion that 'imitation, like
all mental activity, is a process of active, constructive organizing and
structuring of the environment' being an aspect of overall cognitive
functioning rather than a unique process. Further, that the imitative
function undergoes transformations, as the individual develops, the
individual having the capacity to imitate only those behaviours which
are allowed by physical-motor and cognitive maturity.

In conclusion Kuhn emphasized that her position in no way implies
a denial of the role of environmental factors in influencing behaviour

* Gratitude is extended to Professor Deanna Kuhn of California State University
for sending her work to be abstracted. (Now at Harvard University.)

and behaviour change, the issue being not whether the environment affects behaviour, but rather the process by means of which this effect takes place.

*Inducing   development   experimentally: comments   on   a   research paradigm**
D. Kuhn, 1974

Kuhn presented a paper designed to further the discussion of the issues that were raised by Brainerd and Allen (1971) with respect to conservation training studies. Kuhn observed that Brainerd and Allen concluded that the evidence strongly supported the view that conservation can be induced by short-term experimental means. She emphasized however that their sole criterion for success of a training study was the statistical significance of the post-test difference between experimental and control groups on whatever index of conservation the experimenters employed. Kuhn concluded that there are two major questions that must be addressed in evaluating any training study: first, it needs to be decided what the training experience consisted of from the subject's point of view and second, criteria for evaluating the effects of the training experience need to be decided. Even though many training studies have followed Piaget's 1964 criteria for ascertaining whether a researcher has succeeded in teaching operational structures (these criteria have been set out in the review section in this present volume) the evaluation of any training intervention necessarily remains ambiguous. With respect to explanation it needs to be remembered that the subject has already been exposed to explanation in the training procedure and therefore appropriate explanations cannot be considered a sufficient criterion to permit a judgment of genuine change. The duration criterion can likewise be interpreted as a situation where the subject might during a second post-test make the same responses he did during the first post-test because he had interpreted those responses as the desired or correct ones for that situation and further, he found himself in the situation a second time. Kuhn further dismissed countersuggestion as a valid indicator on the grounds that Smedslund (1961b) found that some natural conservers could be influenced to change from conservation to non-conservation judgments. With respect to generalization Kuhn queried the amount of generalization to non-trained items which is necessary to infer genuine structural change.

* Gratitude is extended to Professor Deanna Kuhn of California State University for sending her work to be abstracted. (Now at Harvard University.)

Kuhn further emphasized a related lack of theoretical agreement as to what a conservation judgment reflects as indicated by the diversity of techniques that have beem employed in an attempt to induce conservation. (Kuhn, pp. 594–95).

Following a discussion with respect to the possibility of simulating the conservation process described by Piaget, in a short-term experimental setting (Kuhn, p. 596), Kuhn concluded that every training study should be undertaken as a part of a research programme that has as its foundation a careful longitudinal assessment of the natural development of that concept and any concepts thought to be closely related. (Further details appear in Kuhn, p. 599.)

Training of number conservation in retardates
R.P. Lancaster and D.L. McManis, 1973

AIM / An examination of the effects of a number conservation training procedure was undertaken which combined the cognitive-conflict aspect of Gruen's (1965) and the reversibility aspect of Kaplan's (1967) procedure.

SUBJECTS / N = 18. Three groups of six Ss each were equated on IQ, Stanford-Binet mental age score, and number conservation pre-test score. The IQ ranged from 43 to 69, five years five months to seven years nine months in MA, and from zero to 12 (19 points possible) on the number conservation pre-test.

METHOD / The pre-tests administered were as follows:
(a) More–less test; (b) Number conservation test; (c) Substance conservation test. 'The total group was divided into three subgroups equated for pre-test performance, five weeks of training were carried out with the two treatment groups. The control Ss were not interacted with by E during this period. In the week following the training period, all three groups were given post-tests for number conservation and substance conservation'. The two training procedures were addition–subtraction and reversibility. Fuller details of the tests, including training procedures are described elsewhere, Lancaster and McManis, (1973, pp. 307–310).

RESULTS / The authors conclude, 'Under cognitive-conflict, trans-formation of one of two sets of discrete elements produced a perceptual illusion, and the addition–subtraction and reversibility operations applied to that set produced conflict between its length and density. Under nonconflict, simultaneous application of the operations to both sets avoided such conflict. Both training groups made significant gains from pre-test and significantly exceeded controls in post-test number conservation (ps < .05). Lack of differential gains by the training groups suggested that cognitive conflict is not essential to induce number conservation', p. 303.

*Conservation: Transmitted or Constructed?**
M. Lifschitz and P.E. Langford, 1975

According to Piaget and Inhelder (1941) conservation judgments are learned through three mechanisms: identity (addition—subtraction), compensation and reversibility. These each correspond to a certain line of argument taken by children when asked to justify a conservation judgment. Piaget and Inhelder consider that by reflecting upon his own experience, and particularly his experience of performing trans-formations upon objects and materials, the child arrives at these three forms of justification for a conservation judgment. The problem with their analysis, however, is that it is difficult to see how the child knows that a collection of objects, for instance, contains the same amount before and after a transformation, such as spatial rearrangement. This is essential, as while the above arguments (or at least two of them: addition—subtraction and compensation) are valid when applied to the right kind of situation, the child must first find out what kind of situation to apply them to. It is no good, for instance, applying the addition—subtraction argument to the stretching of a rubber band: we cannot say that because no elastic has been added or removed the band is the same length stretched as unstretched. It would be a correct argument in relation to its weight, but not in relation to its length. To find this out we have to establish a criterion for weight and a criterion for length; then we can find out which transformations of the band affect length and which affect weight. It is argued that the only reliable criteria available to children for deciding whether two magnitudes are equal are counting and measurement, and that in the first instance it is particularly counting that is important.

The only substantial evidence for the existence of Piaget and Inhelder's three mechanisms comes from studies in which the mechanisms have been translated into corresponding methods of training conservation judgments in children. As training methods based upon the mechanisms have proved among the best in inducing

* Written and prepared by the authors for inclusion in this volume. Gratitude is extended to Drs M. Lifschitz, and Peter Langford of Birkbeck College University of London.

conservation beliefs in children it might seem that our strictures are unjustified. There is, however, an essential difference between the mechanisms proposed by Piaget and Inhelder (1941) and their implementation in the form of training procedures. This lies in the introduction, in the training procedures, of methods of establishing equality of magnitudes to the child through either adult judgment (he is told the magnitudes are the same) or through counting (the child is asked to count to establish equality).

In the present study, training methods based on the Piaget and Inhelder mechanisms were used, each method being given in two forms. In one form equality of magnitudes was established by adult judgment, in the other the child was asked to count or measure for himself to establish equality. It was found that not only did the adult judgment method result in less learning than the counting method for all three training techniques, but such learning as was achieved had almost entirely evaporated after three months. The counting groups, on the other hand, continued to maintain a strong lead over the control subjects. It was concluded that while conservation learning takes place through cultural transmission of ideas rather than through construction from personal experience, cultural products must be actively used by the child in order to achieve such transmission, rather than just passively acquired. The child must count for himself; it is not enough simply to be told by an adult.

Attention to stimulus dimensions in the conservation of liquid quantity
P.H. Miller, 1973

AIM / The author was intent to examine the relation between conservation of liquid quantity and attention to relevant and irrelevant stimulus dimensions.

SUBJECTS / N = 80. The sample comprised 36 kindergarten non-conservers (mean age = six years); 21 kindergarten conservers (mean age = six years one month); and 23 third grade conservers (mean age = nine years).

METHOD / Each subject was administered the pretraining, attention task and the conservation of liquid test. All subjects were tested individually and all responses recorded verbatim.

The pretraining was undertaken to make sure the subject understood the questions employed in the attention task and the terms 'some' and 'different'. The subject was shown two red circles and a green circle and asked, 'which two are the same?' and 'which one is different?'. Next the subject was shown a small red circle, a large red square, and a small green square. Questions were 'which two are the same?' 'How?' and

'Are there another two which are the same in some other way?'

The attention task evaluated the relative salience of the height, width and quantity of liquids in two sets of cylindrical plastic beakers. These were hidden by a screen when they were not being used. Each child was given four trials, two trials on each set of beakers. The sets of beakers were alternated over the four trials. 'The first dimension a subject chose on each of the four trials was designated the most salient dimension (or dimensions) for that subject. It was possible to choose height, width, or quantity on each trial. This was level one. On trials three and four, two further levels followed level one. Unlike level one, in which every subject made four responses, in levels two and three, subjects could give different numbers of responses. On each of trials three and four a subject could give from zero to two responses in level two and from zero to nine responses in level three. A subject who was able to give nine responses in level three would respond three times each to height, width, and quantity. Within each dimension this subject would give one "same" response (eg, "same height") and two different responses (eg "different height")', p. 132.

The liquid conservation task was modelled after Piaget, with slight modifications.

(Fuller details of the pretraining, attention task and the liquid conservation task are described in Miller, 1973, pp. 131—133).

RESULTS / Miller discussed her results in terms of Gelman's (1969) study in which attentional training successfully enhanced conservation operativity. She concludes, 'Both kindergarten non-conservers and kindergarten conservers found height most salient. In addition, non-conservers nearly always based their beliefs in non-conservation on height. Conservers (and, to a lesser extent, non-conservers) could also attend to width when there was further questioning. Surprisingly, kindergarten conservers seldom attended to quantity. Third grade conservers found quantity most salient but could easily attend to height and width', p. 129.

Perceptual information in conservation: effects of screening
P.H. Miller and K.H. Heldmeyer, 1975

AIMS / Whether totally screening the liquid would produce a high proportion of conservation responses and whether children of different ages would respond differently to the screen and its removal — as in Frank (1966) study.

SUBJECTS / N = 192 children with mean ages of five years 10

months and six years 10 months.

METHOD / Each S was tested individually. There were three conditions, one with a typical conservation procedure, one with fewer perceptual cues, and one with several levels of reduced perceptual cues. 'In every condition each trial began by establishing that the two standards had the same amount of water. One standard was then produced into a different container and the child was asked, "Do we both have the same amount of water or does one of us have more?" and "How did you figure that out?" In conditions in which the water was poured behind a screen, E's arm and both beakers were screened from the child. After the standard was emptied, it was returned to its spot near the other standard which was still full and visible', p. 589. (Fuller details are given in Miller and Heldmeyer, 1975, pp. 589—590.)

RESULTS / Non-operativity increased in kindergarten Ss as the number of cues increased. However, first grade Ss were affected very little by the perceptual conditions. Miller and Heldmeyer suggested that 'the development of conservation involves several levels, beginning with a concept which can be demonstrated only under facilitating conditions', p. 588. 'The implication for the assessment of conservation is that it is inaccurate . . . to categorize a child as a "conserver" or "non-conserver" on the basis of the standard tests. A more accurate and refined test would consist of a number of items which systematically vary along a scale with full perceptual support for conservation or complete lack of irrelevant cues at one end, and no perceptual support or many irrelevant cues at the other end', p. 592.

Facilitation of conservation of number in young children
P.H. Miller, K.H. Heldmeyer, and S.A. Miller, 1975

AIM / To identify conditions that facilitate conservation of number.

SUBJECTS / N = 64 aged three, four, and five years.

METHOD / Seven trials of number conservation varied in the number and type of perceptual supports. 'Supports included an emphasis on one-to-one correspondence between objects in the two arrays, a reduction of length cues which may draw attention from number, a small number of objects, and stimuli of high interest. The trials, in order of decreasing perceptual support, were (a) four pairs of small plastic animals . . . transformed from pairs randomly placed in a field to a small bunched-up group containing one member of each pair;

(b) same as Trial 1 but with eight pairs; (c) four pairs of animals transformed from pairs randomly placed in a field of two lines of unequal length; (d) four pairs of animals with the transformation of one of two equal lines into a longer line; (e) four pairs of beads of four corresponding colours with the transformation of one of two equal lines into a longer line; (f) four pairs of beads in two rows, one red and one blue, with the transformation of one of two equal lines into a longer line; (g) same as Trial six but with eight pairs. To avoid a response bias of "same", a display with unequal numbers followed the fourth trial. The . . . three-, four-, and five-year-olds formed two conditions which differed in the order of trials — 1 to 7 (easy to difficult) or 7 to 1 (difficult to easy)', p. 253.

RESULTS / The authors argued that it was inaccurate to label young children as simply conservers or non-conservers. Majority of the children were operational under some conditions and non-operational under others. When perceptual supports were provided, 'a rudimentary understanding of conservation is revealed. However, the concept is so fragile that it does not appear under usual testing condition,' p. 253.

Extinction of conservation: a methodological and theoretical analysis
S.A. Miller, 1971

The author was intent to clarify some of the issues involved in the Hall and Simpson (1968) and Smedslund (1968) debate. The former authors argued that conservation can be extinguished while the latter maintained that conservation can never be extinguished. Miller (1971) reviews selected extinction studies.

Smedslund's (1961) objective was to create an additional assessment technique which would permit him to examine the apparent success of a learning-oriented training procedure. One group comprised of 11 children who had been successfully trained in weight conservation. These subjects were compared with 13 children who had demonstrated conservation operativity on the pre-test ('natural conservers'). 'The extinction manipulation consisted of the surreptitious removal, during the conservation transformation, of a piece of clay from one of two initially equal-weight balls, followed by a weighing which demonstrated that the weights were now unequal. The child was asked to explain the inequality, and he was judged to have extinguished if he failed to give a conservation-congruent explanation . . . All 11 trained subjects extinguished by this criterion; in contrast, six of the 13 natural conservers successfully resisted extinction', p. 320. Kingsley and Hall (1967) using identical procedures to Smedslund's study introduced extinction as a check on the success of a conservation training technique. However, Hall and Kingsley (1968) examined the problem of extinction in natural conservers. Sixteen subjects whose conservation pre-test performance had been perfect were presented the extinction manipulation identical to Smedslund's study (*op. cit.*). In a second study, 64 college students were shown the extinction trial in a group situation and asked to write down 'why the two pieces of clay did not weigh the same'. Overall, little evidence of resistance to extinction emerged from either of the Hall and Kingsley studies. Hall and Simpson (1968) were intent to identify experimental variables that might determine whether the child resists or extinguishes. Variables examined were tape-recorded *vs.* live presentation of the task; peer experimenter *vs.* adult experimenter; and the number of alternatives to a non-conservation explanation present in this situation. None of these variables had any effect on resistance, which was uniformly low. They also examined the subject's explanation for the change but also his predictions on subsequent conservation trials within the same session and on a post-test fourteen days later. They also administered disconfirmation-of-beliefs trials not only to conservers but also to non-conservers, who therefore saw conservation and to partial conservers, half of whom saw conservation and half non-conservation.

Subjects in all of these groups demonstrated substantial and equivalent change in their predictions. On the delayed post-test, however, subjects who had observed instances of conservation operativity did appear to have retained more from their previous experience than subjects who had seen the non-conservation outcomes.

Studies which have employed extinction within the framework of conservation training studies include Brison (1966); Brison and Bereiter (1967); Sullivan (1967, 1969); and Smith (1968). These studies suggest that, 'there is almost no evidence that natural conservers are more resistant to extinction than trained conservers. Second, resistance to extinction is low for both natural and trained conservers. Thus, the basis for the two groups' equivalence is not that trained conservers are surprisingly resistant to extinction (a finding which a Piagetian analysis might have been able to incorporate); rather, the groups are equivalent because natural conservers are surprisingly easy to extinguish', p. 322.

Miller puts forward a debate on the problems of assessment and maintains ' . . . such a diagnosis would require that a number of problems employing different transformations be presented, that consistently correct responding to these problems be possible only if the child is a conserver, and that the child not only answers all of the problems correctly but also provide a logical explanation for his answers. Existing studies have met these criteria to varying degrees. Most satisfactory in this respect are the studies by Smedslund (1961),

Brison (1966), and Hall and Simpson (1968). The other four studies which have sought to include natural conservers are open to criticism. In both Kingsley and Hall (1967) and Hall and Kingsley (1968), one of the three conservation assessment trials (the one involving conservation of inequality) is clearly invalid. In Smith (1968), three of the five trials are continuations of the preceding trial, for example, a ball is changed into a sausage, the question is asked, then the sausage is turned into a snake and the question asked again. This procedure is not the standard one, and it may have biased towards repetition of an initial correct answer. Finally, in Sullivan (1967) the description of the conservation test is too sketchy to permit evaluation; it appears, however, that the test was limited to a single trial', p. 324. Miller finally concludes with a critical look at the extinction procedures and theoretical considerations.

Contradiction, surprise, and cognitive change: the effects of disconfirmation of belief on conservers and non-conservers
S.A. Miller, 1973

AIM / An examination of children's reactions to violations of their expectancies concerning conservation of weight was undertaken.

SUBJECTS / N = 69, with an age range from eight years to eleven years. The children were drawn from a middle class suburb of Minneapolis.

METHOD / Non-conservers, young conservers, and old conservers participated in the study. Each of the groups received feedback which consistently disconfirmed its expectancy regarding conservation. The two kinds of reaction were evaluated: expressive response (surprise) and cognitive change. 'Surprise was inferred from videotaped facial reactions, verbalizations, and delays in a reaction — time response contingent upon the outcome (the latter adopted from Charlesworth, 1964; and Charlesworth and Zahn, 1966). Cognitive change was inferred from the child's explanations for the outcomes, his judgments and explanations on a series of generalization trials, and his response to post-test questioning', p. 49. The concept examined was the conservation of weight, and the central piece of apparatus was a hanging-pan balance scale. Alignment or non-alignment of the two pans or the movement of a pointer attached to the scale arm helped in reading the results on the scale. The scale was capable of providing accurate or distorted feedback.
(Fuller details of pretraining and the conservation pre-test; reaction

time and feedback trials; post feedback trials and post-test questioning
are described in Miller, 1973, pp. 51—54.)

RESULTS / Miller concludes, 'Contrary to expectation, observable
surprise proved infrequent in all groups. In contrast, changes in
conservation judgment were frequent, although the degree of change
was reduced somewhat if an appropriate explanation was required. The
three groups were generally indistinguishable in the extent to which
they changed. Evidence of active resistance to change (as defined by
explanations which denied the validity of the outcome) was absent in
non-conservers but appeared in about half the conservers. Older
conservers were no more likely to resist extinction than were younger
conservers', p. 47.

An attempt to extinguish conservation of weight in college students
S.A. Miller, L.C. Schwartz and C. Stewart, 1973

AIM / The authors were intent to examine if conservation could be
extinguished in adults.

SUBJECTS / N = 36. Eighteen male and 18 female undergraduates
took part in the study, with a median age of 20 years one month.

METHOD / A standard pre-test for conservation of weight was
administered. All subjects showed operativity on all four trials. 'Pre-test
was succeeded by three similar problems on which feedback was
provided following the subject's judgment and explanation. The
feedback in each case indicated non-conservation. The subject was
asked to explain the outcomes; questioning continued until he either
appeared satisfied with an answer or was unable to provide anything
further. The session concluded with two post-test trials without
feedback', p. 316.

RESULTS / Whereas Hall and Kingsley's (1968) results demonstrated that most college students will abandon conservation, the
finding of the present study is of strong resistance. 'The results are also
in contrast to those obtained with children. This latter finding suggests
that there may be developmental changes in the certainty with which a
concept such as conservation of weight is held, changes which extend
well beyond the point at which a child is usually considered to "have"
the concept', p. 316. The authors examine and analyze the two main
measures of change: one was the subject's explanations for the
outcomes (e.g., the denials that non-conservation had occurred) and the

other the response to subsequent conservation trials.

*Conservation deductions and ecological validity**
F.B. Murray, 1976

For more than a decade and a half, the conservation problem in young children's reasoning has been the subject of an intensive, although unsystematic and often ritualized, research effort which has yielded a corpus of well over 500 published articles. The solution to the problem itself requires, presumably, a deductive inference from four premises, two of which are explicit in the experimental procedure and two must be supplied implicitly by the subject. The source and development of these implicit premises by the child is the research problem of the conservation research area.

When A is one object and B is another one of the same material, and where x is one property of the objects, such as their weight, or mass, or length, etc. and y is another property of the objects that is independent or not highly correlated with x, such as their form, or colour, etc., and where $\xrightarrow{\quad t \quad}$ indicates that one object is transformed or changed with respect to one of the properties, the explicit premises are:

1. $Axy = Bxy$
2. $Ay \xrightarrow{\quad t \quad} A^1 y$, which results in $Ay \lessgtr A^1 y$

The implicit premises are:

3. $Ax = A^1 x$
4. $A = B, B = C$, therefore $A = C$

The conclusion or deduction, namely $A^1 x = Bx$, is the conservation judgment if it cannot be made solely by inspecting A^1 and B and if it is felt to be necessary. If it can be made by an inspection of A^1 and B, then the judgment is not conservation, but simple perceptual discrimination. It can also be required that the subject support his deduction with an explanation, but this is a troublesome requirement because there is considerable disagreement about what constitutes an adequate justification for the judgment. The appeal to reversibility, for example, is inadequate although it is accepted by many researchers (Murray and Johnson, 1968). While a good many factors are known

* Published with the kind permission of the author.
  Gratitude is expressed to Professor Frank B. Murray of the University of Delaware

now to be related to the conservation deduction, a compelling explanation of the failure to make the deduction or the identification of sufficient conditions for it have eluded researchers in the field. Still it is possible to map out a general functional system of conservation variables, as follows. The ability to make the deduction is related to the child's age, IQ, mental age, socioeconomic status and its correlates, not sex, cognitive style (field independence, analytic) linguistic development, and ethnic origin. In the end, the very best predictor of conservation has turned out to be the child's mental age. A number of task variables have been clearly identified as well. The particular content of the problem, that is the x factor, interacts with the child's presumed competence to make the deduction. The scale of content difficulty appears to be from easiest to most difficult—identity, number, mass and quantity, length, area, weight, time, volume (occupied and displaced) followed by a cluster of contents which are quite difficult, but whose position on the scale, so to speak, is not well established. These are such variables as density, momentum, elasticity, and numerical equivalence, which in at least one case we have researched recently, is very difficult even for adults (Murray and Armstrong, 1975). The particular material of the problem, namely the A and B, are known to be significant factors also. For example, whether the problem refers to the attributes of a person or an inanimate object is significant since we have found that the child conserves his own weight later than he conserves the weight of a clay ball (Murray, 1969). There is some evidence also that the properties of continuous materials are more difficult to conserve than those of discontinuous materials, but more systematic treatment of this variable is needed; we have just completed an elaborate study in which we found no evidence for this difference between continuity and discontinuity of stimulus materials (Murray and Holm, 1975). Familiarity with the material appears also to be a factor, as in the case with Indian pottery-making children who conserve mass, weight, and volume of clay under various transformations earlier than other children. In sum, there exist a number of subject and task variables that affect whether or not the conservation deduction will be made, and these provide the beginning for a general ecological map of the task.

While the conservation task has been over-researched and in some cases mindlessly approached, there remain, nevertheless, a number of interesting and even neglected questions about the task that could profit from an ecological approach whether it be merely a methodological requirement for ecological validity or generalizability, or the more ambitious theoretical requirement that the non-conservation phenomena itself cannot be understood except as a variable in a system in much the same way as a number cannot be understood apart from the system of numbers.

The conservation problem seems ecologically valid in at least two senses. In itself it is often a real-life problem and experimental assessment procedures which have simulated real-life situations have not provided results that differ from more standardized laboratory techniques. Indeed, Piaget's own clinical method, depending as it does on free flowing conversation between the child and experimenter, has for that reason considerable validity, and has yielded results which more rigorous laboratory procedures have replicated with astonishing consistency. Not to put too fine a point on the matter, I can relate two personal instances of non-conservation in the real world, so to speak. In the first, my two younger brothers were in the habit of pooling their pennies to jointly buy Christmas presents, when one morning in the wee hours they poured the pennies from their separate jars into a third jar, and concluded that by this action they had more money. With great excitement they told me of their discovery of a way to increase their wealth and the number and quality of the presents they would give. Nothing I could say dissuaded them from this view. In the second case, some years later, I received a stern admonition from a fellow worker in a meat packing plant not to crumple the meat wrapping paper on the scale because it would increase the weight and foul up the weighings. However, as he was much bigger, I let the matter pass.

The problem is valid in a second sense also in that it provides a general paradigm for what we mean when we understand a concept. To know whether a concept has been understood one may subject one of its exemplars to a number of transformations to determine when the concept has changed or even ceased to be. One can discover one's concept of 'table,' for example, by transforming a table on any number of dimensions until it is no longer a table. Precisely such a procedure was used in the Platonic dialogues in which, for example, the concept of justice or virtue would be assigned to an event which was subsequently transformed to determine whether the concept could still be assigned. Thus, while it is just to repay a debt, is it just to repay it if the repayment will injure the creditor? By such a dialectical procedure, the very concept itself was discovered, constructed, determined and understood.

Turning now to some problems that might be clarified through an ecological approach, one overriding empirical and theoretical problem that remains in our understanding of the conservation deduction, and all reasoning tasks for that matter, is the interaction between the logical structure of the task and the content of the premises (*cf.* Wason and Johnson-Laird, 1972). The conservation deduction may be much more determined by the content aspects of the task, eg., the materials and particular transformations, than by its logical form. Should the relevancy of the transformation be misjudged so that $Ax \leqslant A^1 x$, the non-conservation conclusion is every bit as logical and as necessary a deduction as the conservation deduction. We have, in fact, just completed an investigation in which all non-conservers appreciated the logical structure of the task, *viz.* transitivity of equals, and some felt that their non-conservation conclusion was necessary (Armstrong and Murray, 1975). The theoretical significance of the conservation task in organismic and structural theories will be enhanced by the replication of the conservation stage constancies in many ecological settings in which it can be determined whether or not the conservation deduction is controlled by specific situational factors.

In this regard, the fact of the *horizontal décalage* or the time lags in the manifestation of the various conservations is a considerable threat to a structural view unless a way can be found to segregate some hypothetical competence and performance factors and to attribute the *décalage* to the latter. Egon Brunswick's notion of ecological validity and the intra-ecological correlation may be useful in this connection because the magnitude of the environmental correlations of what we have called the x and y factors may be predictive of the *décalage* sequence (Hammond, 1966). Researchers have neglected to specify the environmental system of the conservation task stimuli so that we do not know what the environmental correlations are between size and weight, height and age or amount, length and number, and so forth. These could be determined as Brunswick determined the correlations between proximal and distal cues or the correlations for the Gestalt organizational principles. Non-conservation is, after all, quite reasonable when x and y are in fact highly correlated.

Moreover, we have no theory of why some conservation transformations are effective, i.e., lead to non-conservation, and some others have no effect. Why is it that a change in an object's temperature is taken as a change which alters weight by first and second graders while a change in the object's position does not? A similar Brunswick analysis of the correlations in the environment between classes of transformations and changes in objects' weight, etc. would be useful. In this connection, we have evidence that indicates that effective conservation transformations are those which change an aspect of an object which is connotatively related to the property to be conserved (Nummedal and Murray, 1969; Murray and Haldas, 1974; Murray and Tyler, 1975). Thus as hard, rough, strong, large are all connotations of the property, heavy, transformations which change an object's hardness, roughness, size, etc. may be taken by children as transformations which change its weight also. We have found this to be the case (Murray and Johnson, in press). In this semantic account of the conservation transformation, the ecological validity, in Brunswick's sense, of the connotations of heavy or light would be important to determine.

A final problem in the conservation literature which might yield to an ecological approach is the question of how the conservations are acquired. While it is beyond the scope of this paper to review the conservation training literature — some several hundred papers in its own right — two points can be made.

The first is that the training literature, enduring vigorously as it has for 15 years with every unhappy sign for a continued life, shows a striking discrepancy between the earlier and later studies. The studies of the early 1960s led reviewers like Flavell (1963) and Sigel (1964) to conclude that conservation was unteachable. A decade later Wolhwill (1970) concluded that this negative result 'has been largely and effectively superseded by a consistent stream of studies reporting much more positive results regarding the effectiveness of a variety of training procedures.' More striking, perhaps, is that many of the later studies, for one reason or another, duplicated the earlier procedures. For example, Gelman's (1969) successful procedure largely duplicates one of Smedlund's unsuccessful ones (1961).

This puzzling state of affairs suggests a cohort effect in the subjects or perhaps the researchers whose theoretical biases changed. On the latter somewhat facetious point, the criteria for conservation often have subtle theoretical differences; for example, the Piagetians often adopt fixed trials criterion measures while the non-Piagetians are more likely to adopt trials to criterion measures. To attribute the discrepancy between the earlier and later studies to a cohort effect, which may be correct, is a weak attribution without a supporting analysis and specification of the ecological factors that may have produced the cohort effect, such as, for example, the pre- and post-Sputnik curriculum reform projects and climate in the United States.

The second and concluding point deals with some training studies we have just completed which illustrate how a quest for ecological validity may legitimately turn back on itself and lead profitably to more artificial and removed investigations. In two experiments (Murray, 1972) we demonstrated that in a social interaction situation, nonconservers who were confronted by conserver's arguments came to adopt conservation in a generalized form when they were tested alone. The finding has been replicated widely (Silverman and Stone, 1972; Silverman and Geiringer, 1973; and Miller and Brownell, 1975). The procedure was thought to simulate real-life interaction in which children who disagree often argue to a resolution where one may either acquiesce or become genuinely convinced. Although it was clear in these studies that non-conservers now conserved, it was never clear just what they learned or what aspects of the global interaction situation were critical for the training effect. It might have been the case that the non-conservers acquired conservation, not through a dialectical process, but by simple imitation of the conservers. Indeed we (Botvin and Murray, 1975) and others (Rosenthal and Zimmerman, 1972; Waghorn and Sullivan, 1970) have evidence that conservation can be acquired by merely observing a conserving model. Why this should be so, when conservation in the earlier studies was so very resistant to some very elaborate and reasonable training procedures is a puzzle.

It may be that what was going on in these social interaction and modeling studies was that the treatments produced a classic cognitive dissonance. Indeed a dissonance procedure is consistent with the equilibration mechanism Piaget has proposed for the acquisition of conservation. So we (Murray and Ames, 1975) asked non-conservers to pretend to conserve, that is to lie — to say they believed A and B were the same when before they had claimed that they were not the same. This they did in front of another child. Conservers pretended not to conserve. The results were clear and striking — conservers were unaffected by the presumed dissonance between what they truly believed and what they said they believed. Non-conservers were greatly affected by the treatment and came to adopt their public position, i.e., they conserved and generalized their responses. In a subsequent study, which replicated the first study, these newly trained nonconservers were also subjected to a second dissonance procedure, and like the natural conservers before they were unaffected by it. Thus, it could very well be the case that the controlling mechanism in the social interaction and subsequent imitation studies was a cognitive dissonance-type mechanism, which was discovered in a quite artificial experimental situation which was designed to simulate a presumed natural course of cognitive motivation — but at a more molecular level.

In sum, while a number of conservation variables of the presumed system have been identified, a number of important theoretical problems remain, and these may yield to an ecological perspective of both method and theory.

Induction of linear-order concepts: a comparison of three training techniques
P.B. Pufall, 1973

AIM / A comparison of three training techniques was undertaken to examine whether any of these facilitated an operational understanding of linear order.

SUBJECTS / N = 55. The Caucasian kindergarten children had a mean IQ of 100.13 on the Peabody Picture Vocabulary Test (Dunn, 1965) and were drawn from lower-middle to middle social class background.

METHOD / Out of the original sample of 55, nine children were excluded from training and post-testing sessions. These children had achieved a pre-set criterion of conservation (correct on 75 per cent of the criterial trials on any task). The remainder of the Ss were randomly assigned to one of the three training conditions.

Pre-tests included (a) Construction, (b) Rotation, and (c) Identification.

The training procedures employed were as follows:

(a) Reciprocity − 'This training essentially duplicated the procedure followed in the construction task. However, shorter sequences were employed ... Reciprocity training gave the child practice in constructing orders identical with (A B C) or the reciprocal of (C B A) a model (A B C)'.

(b) Reversibility − 'This training included reciprocity training and added to it experiences with rotational transformations. Twelve trials identical with reciprocity training alternated with 12 trials of rotational transformations ... training included reciprocity training and experience predicting and observing the outcome of a 135° rotation and its reverse (−135°)'.

(c) Discrimination − 'This training was similar to identification but differed from it in that S could compare a model simultaneously to an identical, a reciprocal, and a different sequence. Discrimination involved sorting the sequences into one of three categories on each of 24 trials ... training required the child to identify pairs of orders as identical, reciprocals, or different (e.g. A B C to A C B)'.

Post-testing was identical to pre-testing and was administered the day after each child completed training.

Fuller details of pre-testing, criterion of conservation, training procedures and post-testing are described in Pufall (1973, pp. 643–644).

RESULTS / All three training techniques demonstrated learning on the part of the children with significant specific transfer effects. However, only reversibility training led to generalized transfer to all three post-testing tasks. Pufall speculates on the effectiveness of reversibility training and argues ' ... is due to the fact that both the transformations of constructing a reciprocal order and predicting the outcome of rotations are structured in the same experience. Perhaps by

incorporating both of these transformational activities into one
experience, the child was provided not only with information about
their relation but also with the incentive to establish an equilibrium
between them . . . The task-specific transfer of the other two training
procedures indicates that children could learn from these experiences
but also reinforces the importance of experiences with varied
transformational activities in the development of operational
understanding', p. 645.

Modeling by exemplification and instruction in training conservation
T.L. Rosenthal and B.J. Zimmerman, 1972

Experiment One
AIM / The response criteria of correct judgment alone, and of
correct judgment and explanation together in conservation operativity
were investigated.

SUBJECTS / N = 100 within the age range from five years nine
months to six years eight months. Equal number of subjects were
assigned to the control group or the experimental conditions.

METHOD / The tasks administered were Forms A and B of the
Goldschmid and Bentler (1968b) Concept Assessment Kit. 'Form A was
given to all children in a base-line phase and, following presentation of
modeling (or control) treatments, it was immediately readministered in
an imitation phase to assess vicariously created (and control) changes.
Directly after, in a generalization phase, Form B was introduced to all
children without further training to determine the transfer of
conservation to new stimulus items. Each child was taken from class to
a separate room where he worked with the adult male experimenter and
the adult female model . . . After base line, experimental subjects were
instructed as follows: 'Now let's give the lady a chance to play the
game. I want you to watch and listen carefully, and you will have a
chance to play the games again later''. The model then performed and,
subsequently, the experimenter retransformed the stimuli out of sight
of the child and then introduced the imitation phase by saying = "*Now,
let's play* these games again" — To assess "Spontaneous" changes
without training, the (italicized, word and italicization inserted) were
given to control subjects directly after base line. Form A was then

readministered and next Form B was presented to all subjects with the following instruction: "Here are some little bit different games for you to play",' p. 393. Under treatments equal number of boys and girls were assigned 'to each of four experimental groups or to no model, control condition. Experimental subjects observed the model give an equivalence judgment to each item of Form A, using three verbal formats to avoid repetition of precise wording: "There's just as much here as is there"; "They're both the same"; or "There is the same amount here as is there". For half of the subjects, the experimenter asked the model to explain her judgment of equivalence. The model then supplied the following rule: "Because they were the same in the first place". Rule provision was omitted for the remaining children. As a second variable, feedback was studied by having feedback groups observe the experimenter verbally reinforce the model ("that's right," "that's good," or "correct") after each of her responses; verbal praise to the model was omitted in no feedback conditions. The four groups formed by combining Rule Feedback treatments each contained 10 boys and 10 girls . . . analyses were separately computed for conservation defined by just equivalence judgments (judgments only), and for the equivalence judgments plus explanation (judgments plus rule) . . . ', p. 394.

Experiment Two

AIM / To determine whether observing a model fail to give conservation judgments would reduce conservation in children, who, originally, had shown evidence of being able to conserve.

SUBJECTS / N = 17 within the age range five years nine months to six-years eight months.

METHOD / The experimental procedure as experiment one was used except if, however, a child judged the transformed stimuli by the judgments only criterion to be equivalent on at least five base-line items, 'he was for training assigned to observe the model demonstrate non-conservation judgments', p. 397.

Experiment Three

AIM / To compare 'the information-transmitting effectiveness of modeling with a non-modeling, verbal rule instructions technique', p. 397.

SUBJECTS / N = 28 Chicago children from an economically depressed area with an age range from six years one month to seven years.

METHOD / Seven boys and seven girls were assigned to each of two experimental treatments: the modelling treatment, as per experiment one and 'a non-modelling instructions variation', After training through modelling or instructions, both groups received the same procedures in the invitation phase retest and, with no further training in the generalization phase.

Experiment Four

AIM / To extend various aims cited above to very young children.

SUBJECTS / N = 13 within the age range from four years two months to four years nine months.

METHOD / The observational training procedure was patterned after Bandura and Harris (1966). ' . . . the model would perform on an item using the procedures of the no rule provision, no feedback condition of Experiment I. Then, the experimenter would return the transformed stimulus member to its original state . . . out of sight of the child, and immediately presented the item to the subject. Thus, the model and child alternated in responding sequentially to the six items of Form A. Subsequently, the generalization phase was . . . introduced without further training and the six Form B items were presented in series with no intervention by the model . . . the experimental procedures were identical with those specified in Experiment I', p. 399.

RESULTS / Rosenthal and Zimmerman conclude, 'Observational learning by middle class Anglo-Americans, by economically disadvantaged Chicano first graders, and by four-year-olds was found in multidimensional conservation tasks. Without further training, imitative conservation was generalized to new stimuli. Verbally praising the model's responses did not affect performance. A non-conserving model reduced initially conserving children's scores. A non-modelling instructions procedure did not alter conservation. Providing a rule to explain stimulus equivalence improved responses when both judged equivalence and explanation were required, but not when judged equivalence alone was observing a model conserve without giving explanations increased correct judgments plus rule responses in imitation, indicative of inferential thinking elicited by modeling', p. 392.

Training communication skills in young children
C.U. Shantz and K.E. Wilson, 1972

AIM / The hypothesis was drawn from Piaget's (1926) work and was formulated as follows: Subjects training on description (DE) and discrimination (DI) tasks would tend to perform at higher levels of such tasks and on transfer tasks when compared to a group of control children.

SUBJECTS / N = 24 ranging in age from seven years four months to eight years three months. The mean ages of the experimental and control groups were seven years eight months and eight years one month, respectively.

METHOD / A standard card to be communicated about, and three comparison cards as the pre-training and post-training test, were used. 'In DE, the speaker was given only the standard card and told that the listener (. . . photograph) wanted to draw it, and . . . needed to be told everything about it. In DI, the speaker identified the differences between the same standard card and comparison cards, was told that the listener only wanted to find the "right" (standard) card among the four, and . . . the subject was to tell as little as possible but just enough to be sure listener could select the right one. Half the control group and half the experimental group were administered a practice set of animal pictures and a test set with the DE first and then DI. A second test set with different geometric shapes was given in the reverse order. The remaining subjects had opposite orders. At post-testing, orders within each set were reversed for each subject . . . At pre-test, the experiment-ers made on-the-spot evaluations of DE and DI performance by the experimental group to form four training trios, each having a subject of high, medium, and low communication ability . . . this provided a peer model of good communication in each group. Each trio met twice a week for six half-hour training sessions. Each subject took alternately the role of speaker, listener—responder, and listener—observer once each session. For training, cards displayed meaningful objects in different colours and sizes in each quadrant. In DE, the listener used a choice board displaying 18 . . . pieces (combinations of objects, colours, and sizes) and a response card . . . In DI, the speaker and listener had duplicate standard and comparison cards', p. 694.

Transfer tasks — This comprised a checkboard divided into six squares and six toys for placement. The child took in turn any one toy and put it on any one square 'while the experimenter turned his back and tried to reproduce the placements from subjects description', p. 695. The second transfer task was patterned after Krauss and Glucksberg (1969) and Krauss and Weinheimer (1964). The third transfer task was adapted from Flavell (1968).

RESULTS / Trained subjects, compared with the control subjects, at post-testing possessed significantly greater useful information and overall evaluation of messages. Moreover, the results demonstrated that a moderate transfer of skills was also evident.

Compensation and combinatorial systems in the acquisition and generalization of conservation
J.L. Sheppard, 1974

AIM / A training study of conservation was undertaken to investigate whether learning of compensation could be utilized to develop conservation and lead to generalization.

SUBJECTS / N = 80 with an age-range from five to six years.

METHOD / The subjects were selected on the basis of low scores on a conservation pre-test and were randomly assigned to various groups as follows: (a) quantity training — experimental group, (b) substance training — experimental group, (c) matrix training — control group, (d) no training — control group. 'If on the pre-test a S gave any correct responses (without considering explanations) to conservation of quantity as well as conservation of substance (the areas to be trained), he was eliminated from further involvement . . . and testing was . . . discontinued. Generally, if a S gave any correct response to any three conservation . . . the pre-test was discontinued and the S rejected from the experiment. The only exceptions were two Ss in the matrix training-control group and two Ss in the quantity training group who did have at least one correct response on each of three conservation areas', p. 720.

The experimental groups were administered training sessions, one with water containers, one with plasticine, while one control group had experiences with multiplication of relations in a matrix of beakers with no water, and another received no training.

The areas tested comprised quantity, substance, number, length, weight and volume. Post-tests were administered. (Fuller details of the experimental procedure including the training sessions are described elsewhere, Sheppard, 1974, pp. 720—723.)

RESULTS / The author discusses the results with those of Bruner (1966); Sigel, Roeper and Hooper (1966); Bearison (1969); Gelman (1969) and Lister (1972). (Some of these studies have been fully described in Modgil, 1974). The resultant patterns demonstrated that 'A significant number of experimental Ss acquired the conservation involved and generalized in post-tests to other conservations, but in almost all instances control Ss did not change. Practice in the anticipation — of — levels type of task leading to compensation in a structured system such as a groupoid for conservation was effective in producing concept acquisition', p. 717.

The child's concept of horizontality with water levels: a training study
J.L. Sheppard, 1974a

AIM / A training study was conducted into the child's concept of horizontality with water levels.

SUBJECTS / N = 60 non-operational children on the concept of horizontality, selected from an initial sample of 215 from grades two and three.

METHOD / During the first week Ss were given the horizontality pre-test one. 'Two weeks later the horizontality test was given a second time (Pre-test Two). Those Ss with scores of three or more on either of the two horizontality pre-tests were eliminated, the three groups were established by the use of random numbers, and Ss in the experimental group were tested individually for their understanding of a mathematical cyclic two-group and four-group. Training sessions were administered to experimental and control training group Ss usually within the week following the second horizontality pre-test . . . On the completion of training all three groups of Ss were given the first horizontality post-test, which was the same as the pre-tests. For the training groups the testing was done later on the day of the training session. One week later (week five, . . .) all three groups were given a second horizontality post-test. One week later (week six . . .) all three groups received a third horizontality post-test', pp. 193—194 (Fuller details of the horizontality test; training methods: experimental group; training methods; control training group; testing the mathematical two-group and four-group are given in Sheppard, 1974a, pp. 194—195.)

RESULTS / Subjects in the experimental group improved significantly with training, the controls did not. Horizontality post-test scores of the experimental group were found to correlate .5 and .6 with their scores on a previously administered test of mathematical groups (Sheppard, 1974). However, some Ss who showed enhanced performance after training were observed to confuse the horizontal with the vertical: such confusion was interpreted by the author as an indication that subject was approaching operativity.

Concrete operational thought and developmental aspects of solutions to a task based on a mathematical three-group
J.L. Sheppard, 1974b

AIMS / To examine the performance of children at the stage of concrete operations for their learning of a mathematical three group, rotations of an equilateral triangle and the Piagetian tasks.

SUBJECTS / N = 25 within the age range from six to 10 years and an IQ range from 99 to 103 on the Peabody Picture Vocabulary Test (Dunn, 1965).

METHOD / Three tasks comprised the mathematical group. In the first task the subject was presented with a combination of two cards which were laid adjacently to one another and required to state what would be the resultant of the combination. 'He could do this by choosing the appropriate card from a set of three laid out on the table before him. Categorizing the cards "Around and back again" = a, "Next circle − with watch drawing" = b, "Next circle − with watch crossed out" = c, the nine combinations of two cards presented for the nine items, which were administered in a random order, were aa, ab, ac, ba, bb, bc, ca, cb, and cc'. The second mathematical group task consisted of a wooden green circle, three small housed coloured black, white, and red and the placement of a small plastic man at one of the houses. The three cards read, 'Go right around', 'Clockwise to nearest house', and 'Anticlockwise to nearest house'. The test consisted of nine items made up of nine combinations of the cards. The third task consisted of a cardboard equilateral triangle with one corner tip coloured red. 'The triangle could be rotated and the red corner used as a reference point to observe the messages of three cards which read "Don't move", "Next corner like a clock", "Next corner not like a clock". The nine items of what are referred to as the triangle test were made up from the combinations of the cards . . . ', p. 118.

The nine Piagetian tasks included conservation of quantity, substance, number, length and weight together with seriation, cross-classification, horizontality, and transitivity.

Testing programme was divided into six phases. Subjects were given several learning sessions covering phases one, two, and three followed by the mathematical group and operativity tasks which were administered in phases four, five, and six.

(Details of the procedures of the six phases are described in Sheppard, 1974b, pp. 118—119).

RESULTS / The author concludes, 'Except for an initial phase in which the fundamentals of the task were learned, the six-year-olds were significantly inferior to the older children in their success on learning to combine two rotations, learning to replace combinations by a third element, and being able to retain their skill with a closed mapping when tested on the learning material and on transfer material. Operativity correlated with performance on all the tasks of the mathematical group except for the initial preparatory phase. The data were seen as supporting the conclusion that if concrete operations can be described by groupings, operational subjects can establish closure in a mathematical group', p. 116.

Inducing cognitive development and learning: a review of short-term training experiments I: the organismic developmental approach
S. Strauss, 1972

The paper reviewed those studies which have attempted to induce structural transformations (development) and structural elaboration (learning) and to assess the consequences of their findings for a theory of cognitive development. The review was limited to those studies which have attempted to induce these changes from the intuitive to the concrete operations stages. Methodological problems for this intent included stage assessment procedures and criteria; the assessment of transitional subjects; and the fit between some studies theoretical aims and research strategies. The categories of the research methodology were consistent with the 'organismic—developmental' approach.

The kinds of training focused upon included disequilibrium, mental operations and regression. It was concluded that despite the centrality of equilibration in Piaget's theory of structural development, four studies have been conducted with the purpose of or which meet the criteria for inducing organizational disequilibrium. 'The major evidence we have that training studies of this type might be successful has been accumulated in a *post hoc* manner. This area seems to have considerable potential for generating research with other than *post hoc* analyses which can produce data which are relevant to organismic stage hypotheses'. Strauss further elaborated: 'If we find conceptual change, we conclude that there was structural disequilibrium. On the other hand, we define disequilibrium as a source of change. In defining elements of the system by each other, we cannot come very close to satisfactory explanations of cognitive advance. This suggests a need for a measure of disequilibrium which is independent of structural change. This motivation should serve as a guide for future investigations'.

'The two strategies in the mental operations type of training include the inducement of mental operations that are characteristic of one stage more advanced than the child's current level of competence, together with the hypothesis that underlying the intuitive stage is a structure whose operational components are segregated, the research strategy being to induce operational integration since an integrated structure is thought to underlie concrete operational reasoning.' From a review of relevant studies (Strauss, pp. 341—45), Strauss concluded that the former strategy was quite unsuccessful while the latter was markedly successful in inducing structural transformation and elaboration. (Further discussion with respect to this conclusion can be found, pp. 345—46.) Findings support the organismic—developmental model's hypothesis that regression to a formerly predominant structure is unlikely, but could result if the structure were not consolidated at a particular level.

Strauss summarized that 'research consistent with the organismic—developmental approach has considerable potential to resolve or better define outstanding theoretical issues'.

A reply to Brainerd
S. Strauss, 1974

Strauss (1974) replies to Brainerd's (1973) review in which the latter criticizes the former's (1972) article entitled, 'Inducing cognitive development and learning: a review of short-term training experiments I: the organismic-developmental approach'. The 30 page reply is summarized by Strauss as follows:

'Brainerd concluded with a set of seven summary statements which he believed were consistent with training study data . . . I will not always quote him directly and will paraphrase some of his points and briefly present a summarizing rejoinder to them.

1. Training treatments which introduce disequilibrium into the cognitive system from external sources have been successful.

This . . . refers to what had been termed adaptational disequilibrium. Of the types of such disequilibrium (prediction-outcome conflict, verbal feedback, conformity, observational learning and dimensional discrimination learning), only conformity training met the criterion of success offered by Brainerd. There have been so few studies of this nature that strong conclusions of the type offered by Brainerd should be tempered.

2. Ss who evidence a given concrete operational concept on the pre-tests tend to be more susceptible to training experiences designed to induce that concept than subjects who do not evidence the concept on the pre-tests. This fact, in and of itself, permits no further conclusions about "structural mixture" and training susceptibility.

This category pertains to organizational disequilibrium . . . Brainerd had claimed that the issue here was one of competence versus performance and that Brainerd's definitions of these notions and their relations to concepts was quite unclear . . . the question seemed to be whether one should accept only *de novo* structural development (as Brainerd would have it) or both structural development and elaboration (as I had claimed).

3. If we have two concrete operational concepts A and B such that A invariably precedes B during the course of normal cognitive growth, A probably will prove easier to train than B in subjects who possessed neither concept. . . . Suffice it to say that the notion of structural mix has little to do with this (*cf.* Strauss and Ilan, in press).

4. Training treatments for a single operation (rule) have successfully induced conservation concepts, especially in the case of inversion reversibility and to a lesser extent for addition—subtraction, identity and reciprocity reversibility.

. . . more careful readings of those articles claimed by Brainerd to support the above position lead one to exactly the opposite conclusions.

5. There is no definitive evidence that multiple operations training will induce conservation, in part because it is confounded with inversion training. In view of statement 4, however, it seems reasonable to suppose that multiple operations training eventually will prove successful also.

Since it had been shown that statement 4 was incorrect, multiple operations training may very well be an interesting avenue of research to follow, but not for the reasons offered by Brainerd. One way to test this idea was suggested by Brainerd . . . to factorially compare multiple operations with individual operations training.

6. The resistance of conservation concepts to extinction treatments is neither universally low nor universally high. Instead, resistance appears to vary as a function of the order emergence of conservation concepts.

Resistance to 'extinction' was shown to have little to do with the order of emergence of conservation concepts. Earlier developing concepts such as discontinuous quantity conservation were no more resistant to 'extinction' than weight conservation . . . concepts emerging at approximately the same time were not equally resistant.

7. To date, appreciable differences in the extinction resistance of trained and natural conservers have not been observed.

It was argued . . . that this may be a function of the testing procedures. Strauss, Danziger and Ramati (1974) found that college students understood what experiments have thought was weight conservation extinction to be related to laws of the operating of the lever. If these findings could be replicated, Brainerd's statement would then be incorrect ... Thus, my original assessment of the training literature seems to me to be sustained', (*ibid.*, pp. 180—1).

Effects of organizational disequilibrium training on structural elaboration
S. Strauss and I. Rimalt, 1974

AIMS / The authors formulated four hypotheses as follows: (a) That significantly more operational discontinuous quantity than intuitive discontinuous quantity Ss would conserve for area after training; (b) To determine the facilitating, debilitating, or neutral influence of concepts not brought into conflict on the conflicting partial structures; (c) the effect of partial structure discrepancy training on concepts not brought into conflict; (d) That for discontinuous quantity, length, and continuous quantity, the order of decreasing stability would be the operational, intuitive, and transitional states.

SUBJECTS / N = 100 children, 60 experimental and 40 control. For both groups of Ss, there were four pre-test operational levels: (a) intuitive for discontinuous quantity, length, continuous quantity, and area; (b) operational or transitional for discontinuous quantity and intuitive for length, continuous quantity, and area; (c) operational for discontinuous quantity; operational, transitional, or intuitive for length; intuitive for area; and (d) operational for discontinuous quantity; operational or transitional for length; operational or transitional for continuous quantity; and intuitive for area.

METHOD / Pre-test was administered to all Ss. Depending on the S's structural profile, he was randomly assigned to either an experimental or control group. Ss in the experimental group were given two post-tests, one soon after training and one 14 days later after the first post-test. The Ss in the control group were administered a post-test two to three weeks after the pre-test. Under the pre-test phase the tasks administered were the discontinuous quantity, length, continuous quantity and area. Each S was administered two items per concept except for area in which one item was administered. The general format was patterned after the Geneva school. In the first part of the training, an attempt was made to have the Ss alternately apply reasoning for discontinuous quantity and for area. The second part of the training procedure was the same as the first, apart from slight modifications in the stimuli used. The post-test items were identical to the pre-test conservation tasks with minor alterations, e.g., two area conservation tasks were administered instead of one. (Full details of the experimental procedures including the training phases and scoring techniques are described elsewhere, Strauss and Rimalt, 1974, pp. 527–529.)

RESULTS / Training was more effective within and between concepts for Ss with 'structural mix' than for those who had no measured 'structural mix'. ' . . . the number of Ss acquiring an ontogenetically later concept increased as a function of increasing pre-test structural elaboration of ontogenetically earlier concepts . . . structural application disruption for earlier concepts impeded acquisition of later concepts; and . . . acquisition of later developing concepts influenced structural elaboration of earlier developing concepts', Strauss and Rimalt, 1974, p. 526.

*Verbal training and development of concrete operations in adult mental retardates**
D. Svendsen, 1973

AIM / To develop concrete operations in a group of adult mental retardates 'in which the cognitive development had ceased'.

SUBJECTS / N = 36. The mean chronological age for the 10 women and eight men in the experimental group was 36 years and the mean chronological age for the nine women and nine men in the control group was 35 years eight months. The average mental age of the experimental group was five years five months and the average mental age of the control group was five years four months on the Columbia Mental Maturity Scale. The groups were equated with respect to CA, MA and performance on four Piagetian tasks.

METHOD / Ten training sessions were administered to the experimental group. 'The subjects were only given one type of tasks from a test of transitivity of length. A subject may be said to possess a capacity for making a transitive inference if he is able to conclude from $A > B$ and $B > C$ to $A > C$'. The training task consisted of the measurement of two pairs of sticks and drawing a transitive inference about the two measured sticks. 'The experimenter gave a correct verbalization of each measurement and the subject was immediately asked to repeat the experimenter's verbalization. The subject's answer was always given a positive or a negative reinforcement and then the experimenter

* Gratitude is extended to Dr D. Svendsen of the University of Bergen for sending his work to be abstracted.

repeated the correct verbalization. The subject's memory for the measurements in each pair was then tested and the subject's answers were once again re-inforced. Then the experimenter repeated the correct verbalization. After this the subject was asked for a transitive inference about the length of the measured sticks'.

The control subjects were administered the Wechsler Preschool and Primary Scale of Intelligence (WPPSI).

Post-test was given to each subject seven to 14 days after the training sessions.

RESULTS / Subjects in the experimental group showed a significant improvement on the transitivity of length test ($p < 0.001$). The effect lasted on the post-test administered three months later and on another post-test two years after the training ($p < 0.01$, $p < 0.02$). Improvement was observed in making transitive inferences and verbal explanations about the inferences. However, subjects in the the control group did not show any enhancement in their performance on the Piagetian tasks.

A developmental study of Piaget's groupement model of the emergence of speed and time concepts
N. Weinreb and C.J. Brainerd, 1975

AIM / To examine some predictions from Piaget's (1970, 1971a, 1971b) analysis of the emergence of speed and time concepts during middle childhood.

SUBJECTS / N = 93 from first, second, and third grades and ranging in age from six to nine years.

METHOD / The Ss were tested on the following: Groupement I speed operations (nested spatial intervals) — The composition and reverse operations were assessed in random order. Groupement V speed operations (spatial order) — The composition and reverse operations were assessed in random order. Groupement I time operations (temporal intervals) and Groupement V time operations (temporal order) — in both the composition and reverse operations were assessed in random order. (Full details of the experimental procedures are given in Weinreb and Brainerd, 1975, pp. 179—181.)

RESULTS / That the respective composition and reverse operations of two of the eight structures posited in the groupement model (Groupement I and Groupement V) should emerge synchronously in each of the two concept areas was not substantiated. Likewise, that the two structures themselves should emerge synchronously in each of the two concept areas was not upheld. That between the two concept areas, the two structures should both emerge in the speed area before either emerges in the time area was only partly supported.

Development and training of time concepts in young children
P.L. Ziegenfuss, 1973

AIM / The author was intent to examine the development and training of time concepts in young children. Piaget's research formed the theoretical basis for the study.

SUBJECTS / N = 100 girls for the standardization sample with an age range from three years ten months to eight years seven months. N = 105 kindergarten boys for the training programme.

METHOD / For the standardization sample a time concept test was developed with three parts: seriation, duration, and coordination. A Kuder-Richardson 20 split-half reliability for the time concepts test total score was .98; short-term (14 days) test—retest reliability was .74, and long-term (five month) test—retest reliability was .82. For the training programme sample 'the concept of time was broken down into its component parts, and tasks were designed by the writer to teach these simpler ideas. The designated tasks were used as group and free play time during the regular kindergarten programme for two experimental classrooms, while the control classrooms continued their normal activities. Over the ten training days the children had about twenty minutes per day of training during group time and about fifteen minutes per day during free play time. The actual training was done by the classroom teachers after receiving instructions from the experimenter. Half of the children in both the experimental and control classes were pre-tested. All of the children were post-tested to determine the effects of training, social class, sex, teacher, pre-test, and order of presentation of the testing items'.

RESULTS / The time concept test data revealed that both CA and social class differences were statistically significant on the total score and the three subtests. The scores substantiated the developmental aspect of time concepts: a consistent increase in scores from pre-kindergarten to second grade. In pre-test there were no significant differences between the treatment groups (experimental or control), sex, or order of testing. Middle class subjects scored significantly higher on all measures except duration. Teacher variable was significant on the coordination measure. In post-test, the treatment effect was significant on all measures, with the experimental subjects performing at the higher levels than the control subjects. Middle class children scored higher than the lower class children. Training was more effective for girls than boys.

Ziegenfuss concludes that training was effective on the time concepts and that such training could be undertaken by classroom teachers.

Modification of young children's grouping strategies: the effects of modeling, verbalization, incentives and age
B.J. Zimmerman, 1974

Experiment One

AIM / The author was intent to investigate 'the vicarious transmission of a conceptual set for grouping stimuli and the child's ability to apply newly acquired sets along with previously held sets on a novel task', p. 1033.

SUBJECTS / N = 68, the three-year-olds ranged in age between three and three years eight months; the four-year-olds ranged in age between four years and four years nine months; and the five-year-olds ranged in age between five years and five years nine months.

METHOD / Briefly, there was 'a no-model control group and four training groups: explanations and incentives, explanations and no incentives, no explanations and incentives, and no explanations and no incentives. All training groups were exposed to a model who responded to the cards according only to the size stimulus dimension. The effects of this training and the ability of the child to integrate this training with prior experience were assessed on a novel generalization task', p. 1036. (Fuller details of the experimental procedures are described elsewhere, Zimmerman, 1974, pp. 1034–1036.)

Experiment Two

AIM / To determine 'whether the inability of the younger children to reverse the grouping set created by the model was an inherent limitation of their intellectual structure or whether this failure was ameliorable through restructuring the model's performance', p. 1038.

SUBJECTS AND METHOD / A second group of four-year-old Ss was assigned to a reversal training condition. These Ss were tested during baseline, generalization, and retention, as in experiment one. 'During training, these youngsters were trained in identical fashion to those children in the no-incentive, model-explanation condition of experiment one with one addition: after the model had initially responded according to the size dimension and the child had imitated, the E turned back to the model and asked (with regard to the same pictures), "Are there any other or different ways these cards are the same?" The model then grouped the cards according to the object—identity stimulus dimension. Then the E asked the model, "Why are they the same?" and the model responded, "Because these are both (object name) and these are both (object name)." The child was then asked the identical questions and given feedback concerning the accuracy of his imitation of the model's object-identity dimension responses', p. 1039.

RESULTS / Brief observation of the model was effective in producing significant generalization and retention of a size-dimension grouping strategy. Although the model's explanations significantly helped acquisition, incentives failed to enhance performance. The S's CA influenced performance; three- and four-year-old Ss who were subjected to a model's size-dimension grouping responses failed to group stimuli according to an initially used object-identity dimension. Subjects aged five were able to use both dimensions. A special training procedure, however, in which the model grouped according to both stimulus dimensions did induce in four-year-olds to utilize both grouping strategies simultaneously.

Conserving and retaining equalities and inequalities through observation and correction
B.J. Zimmerman, and T.L. Rosenthal, 1974

AIM / The authors were intent to study the effects of modeling and corrective feedback on the conservation of equalities and inequalities with items covering three stimulus dimensions (length, number and two-dimensional space).

SUBJECTS / N = non-conservers with a mean age of five years seven months. Six boys and six girls were randomly assigned to each factorial combination of treatments. A female student served as the experimenter and another as the model.

METHOD / Items were selected and modified from the Goldschmid and Bentler (1968b) Concept Assessment Kit. Three sets of stimuli were prepared — each set comprised 12 items, four of which pertained to conservation of length, of number, and of two-dimensional space, respectively. The first stimulus set which assessed length conservation comprised equality and inequality items. The next four items of set one assessed number. Conservation also consisted of equality and inequality items, as did the last four items of set one which assessed conservation of two-dimensional space. Stimulus set two was identical to set one, with similar randomization of presentation sequence, counterbalancing, and distinctions between equality and inequality items. However, 'the number conservation . . . came first' followed by conservation of two-dimensional space and then the items which assessed length conservation. Set three was identical in construction to the first two sets and in terms of random presentation sequences, counterbalancing of item attributes and types and numbers of items. However, the first stimuli assessed two-dimensional space, next stimuli the conservation of length followed by the assessment of number conservation. Set three stimuli were employed in the immediate transfer phase. *Training variations* — Each child was tested individually. For equality items the verbal instructions were similar to Goldschmid and Bentler (1968b) eg, 'Here are a red and a blue stick. They are both the same length. The red stick is just as long as the blue stick. Now watch. (The experimenter performed the transformation.) Now are both sticks the same length or is one longer?' Minor alternations were made in the inequality items, e.g., 'Here are a red and a blue stick. The red stick is longer than the blue stick. Now watch what I do. (The experimenter transformed the stimuli.) Now are both sticks the same length or is one longer?' Both experimenter and the model were present throughout all testing. A child who failed on equality items participated in the training session.

In the 'modelling and explanation' condition, 'the model demonstrated a correct judgment and justified this judgment with a statement of the conservation rule. Children were told to watch while the model played the game. Verbal correction training combined positive feedback for acceptable answers with verbal rule provision . . . children were treated in a manner similar to baseline, but when they judged correctly, they were told "that's right". When they judged an equality item wrongly, they were told, 'They may look different but they were both the same length (had the same amount) in the first place and they still are the same length (have the same amount)". When an inequality item was misjudged, the experimenter explained, "whatever they look like, they don't have the same amount because . . . that one had more in the first place". Thus both the modelling and the correction condition provided the child with a statement of the conservation rule', p. 262. In the 'modelling-plus-correction' condition, subjects first watched the model perform (as above). Then the subject tried each modeled item, and when he was correct he was given positive feedback. However, when he was incorrect, he was instructed as in the verbal correction treatment. Control condition subjects received the set two items without observing the model or obtaining any verbal information.

To measure concept transfer, each child was administered the stimuli as in set three.

(Fuller details of all the tests, experimental procedures, and the scoring techniques are described in Zimmerman and Rosenthal, 1974, pp. 261–263.)

RESULTS / The authors conclude, 'Brief observation of a model, briefer correction training (joining positive feedback with verbal rule provision), and the combination of observation and correction were all successful in producing learning and, without further training, transfer and retention of conservation. Unlike the control (who also never correctly answered any equality items), the trained, experimental groups gave evidence of spontaneously generalizing their new learning to a task that required non-verbal behaviour to manifest conservation', p. 260.

ABBREVIATIONS USED IN THE BIBLIOGRAPHY
(under the series *Piagetian Research*, Vols. 1–8)

Acta Psychol.	Acta Psychologica (Holland)
Adol.	Adolescence
Aging and Hum. Develop.	Aging and Human Development
Alberta J. Ed. Res.	Alberta Journal of Educational Research
Am. Ed. Res. Assoc.	American Educational Research Association
Am. Ed. Res. J.	American Educational Research Journal
Am. J. Ment. Def.	American Journal of Mental Deficiency
Am. J. Orthopsych.	American Journal of Orthopsychiatry
Am. J. Psych.	American Journal of Psychology
Am. J. Soc.	American Journal of Sociology
Am. Psych.	American Psychologist
Am. Psych. Assoc.	American Psychological Association
Am. Soc. Rev.	American Sociological Review
Ann. Rev. Psych.	Annual Review of Psychology
Arch. Dis. Child.	Archives of the Diseases of Childhood (UK)
Archiv. Gen. Psychiat.	Archives of General Psychiatry
Arch. de Psychol.	Archives de Psychologie
Aust. J. Psych.	Australian Journal of Psychology
Aust. J. Soc. Issues	Australian Journal of Social Issues
Brit. J. Clin. & Soc. Psych.	British Journal of Clinical and Social Psychology
Brit. J. Ed. Psych.	British Journal of Educational Psychology
Brit. J. Psych.	British Journal of Psychology
Brit. J. Stat. Psych.	British Journal of Statistical Psychology
Brit. J. Psych. Stat.	British Journal of Psychology – Statistical Section
Brit. J. Soc.	British Journal of Sociology
Brit. Med. Bull.	British Medical Bulletin
Brit. J. Med. Psych.	British Journal of Medical Psychology
Bull. Danish Inst. for Ed. Res.	Bulletin of the Danish Institute for Educational Research
Calif. J. Ed. Res.	Californian Journal of Educational Research
Can. Educ. Res. Dig.	Canadian Educational and Research Digest
Can. J. Behav. Sci.	Canadian Journal of Behavioural Science
Can. J. Psych.	Canadian Journal of Psychology
Can. Psychol.	Canadian Psychology
Child. Developm.	Child Development (USA)
Child Study Journ.	Child Study Journal
Childhood Psych.	Childhood Psychology (UK)
Cogn.	Cognition
Cogn. Psych.	Cognitive Psychology
Contemp. Psych.	Contemporary Psychology (USA)
Dev. Psych.	Developmental Psychology (USA)

Diss. Abstr.	Dissertation Abstracts (USA)
Educ. of Vis. Handicap.	Education of the Visually Handicapped
Educ. & Psych. Measmt.	Educational and Psychological Measurement (USA)
Ed. Res.	Educational Research (UK)
Ed. Rev.	Educational Review (UK)
Educ. Stud. Maths.	Educational Studies in Mathematics
El. Sch. J.	Elementary School Journal (USA)
Eug. Rev.	Eugenics Review (UK)
Excep. Child.	Exceptional Children
Forum Educ.	Forum Education
Gen. Psych. Mon.	Genetic Psychological Monographs (USA)
Harv. Ed. Rev.	Harvard Educational Review
Human Developm.	Human Development (Switzerland)
Hum. Hered.	Human Heredity
Inst. Child Welf. Monogr.	Institute of Child Welfare Monographs
Int. J. Psych.	International Journal of Psychology (France)
Int. Rev. Educ.	International Review of Education (Germany)
Int. Soc. Sci. Bull.	International Social Science Bulletin (France)
Jap. J. Ed. Psych.	Japanese Journal of Educational Psychology
Jap. Psych. Res.	Japanese Psychological Research
J. Abnorm. Soc. Psych.	Journal of Abnormal and Social Psychology (USA)
Journ. Amer. Acad. Child Psychiat.	Journal of American Academy of Child Psychiatry
J. Am. Stat. Assoc.	Journal of American Statistical Association
J. App. Psych.	Journal of Applied Psychology (USA)
J. Compar. Psychol.	Journal of Comparative Psychology
J. Comp. and Physiolog. Psych.	Journal of Comparative and Physiological Psychology
J. Child Psych. Psychiatr.	Journal of Child Psychology and Psychiatry
J. Clin. Psych.	Journal of Clinical Psychology (USA)
J. Consult. Psych.	Journal of Consultant Psychology (USA)
J. Cross. Cult. Psych.	Journal of Cross-Cultural Psychology (USA)
J. Ed. Psych.	Journal of Educational Psychology (USA)
J. Ed. Res.	Journal of Educational Research (USA)
J. Ed. Stud.	Journal of Educational Studies (USA)
J. Exp. Child Psych.	Journal of Experimental Child Psychology (USA)
J. Exp. Educ.	Journal of Experimental Education
J. Exp. Psych.	Journal of Experimental Psychology

J. Gen. Psych.	Journal of Genetic Psychology (USA)
J. Gerontol	Journal of Gerontology
J. Home Econ.	Journal of Home Economics
Journ. Learn. Disabil.	Journal of Learning Disabilities
J. Math. Psych.	Journal of Mathematical Psychology
J. Ment. Sub.	Journal of Mental Subnormality
J. Negro Ed.	Journal of Negro Education (USA)
J. Pers.	Journal of Personality (USA)
J. Pers. Soc. Psych.	Journal of Personality and Social Psychology (USA)
J. Pers. Assessm.	Journal of Personality Assessment (USA)
J. Psych.	Journal of Psychology (USA)
J. Res. Maths. Educ.	Journal of Research in Mathematics Education
J. Res. Sci. Teach.	Journal of Research in Science Teaching (USA)
J. Soc. Iss.	Journal of Social Issues (USA)
J. Soc. Psych.	Journal of Social Psychology (USA)
J. Soc. Res.	Journal of Social Research
J. Spec. Ed.	Journal of Special Education (USA)
Journ. Struct. Learn.	Journal of Structural Learning
J. Teach. Ed.	Journal of Teacher Education (USA)
J. Verb. Learn. Verb. Behv.	Journal of Verbal Learning and Verbal Behaviour (UK/USA)
J. Youth Adolesc.	Journal of Youth and Adolescence
Math. Teach.	Mathematics Teacher (USA)
Maths. Teach.	Mathematics Teaching
Merr.-Palm. Quart.	Merrill-Palmer Quarterly (USA)
Mon. Soc. Res. Child Dev.	Monographs of the Society for Research in Child Development (USA)
Mult. Beh. Res.	Multivariate Behavioural Research
New Zealand Journ. Educ. Stud.	New Zealand Journal of Educational Studies
Ped. Sem.	Pedagogical Seminary
Pedag. Europ.	Pedogogica Europaea
Percep. Mot. Skills	Perceptual and Motor Skills
Psych. Absts.	Psychological Abstracts
Psych. Afric.	Psychologica Africana
Psych. Bull.	Psychological Bulletin (USA)
Psych. Iss.	Psychological Issues
Psych. Mon.	Psychological Monographs (USA)
Psych. Mon. Gen. and Appl.	Psychological Monographs: General and Applied (USA)
Psychol. Rec.	Psychological Record
Psych. Rep.	Psychological Reports (USA)
Psych. Rev.	Psychological Review (USA)
Psychol. Sch.	Psychology in Schools
Psych. Sci.	Psychological Science (USA)
Psychomet.	Psychometrika
Psy.-nom. Sc.	Psychonomic Science
Psy. Today	Psychology Today
Publ. Opin. Quart.	Public Opinion Quarterly (USA)

Quart. J. Exp. Psych.	Quarterly Journal of Experimental Psychology (UK/USA)
Rev. Educ. Res.	Review of Educational Research
R. Belge de Ps. Ped.	Review Belge de Psychologie et de Pédagogie (Belgium)
Rev. Suisse Psych.	Revue Suisse de Pschologie (Switzerland)
Scan. J. Psych.	Scandinavian Journal of Psychology
Sch. Coun. Curr. Bull.	Schools Council Curriculum Bulletin
Sch. Sci. Maths.	School Science and Mathematics
Sci.	Science
Sci. Americ.	Scientific American
Sci. Ed.	Science Education (USA)
Scot. Ed. Stud.	Scottish Educational Studies
Sem. Psychiat.	Seminars in Psychiatry
Soc. Psychi.	Social Psychiatry
Soviet Psych.	Soviet Psychology
Teach. Coll. Contr. Ed.	Teachers' College Contributions to Education (USA)
Theo. into Pract.	Theory into Practice
Times Ed. Supp.	Times Educational Supplement
Train. Sch. Bull.	Training School Bulletin
Vita. Hum.	Vita Humana
WHO Mon.	World Health Organization Monographs
Wiener Arb. z. pad. Psychol.	Wiener Arbeiten zur pädagogischen Psychologie (Austria)
Yearbook Journ. Negro Educ.	Yearbook of the Journal of Negro Education
Zeitschr. f. ang. Psychol.	Zeitschrift für angewandte Psychologie und Charakterkunde (Germany)
Zeitschr. f. pad. Psychol.	Zeitschrift für pädagogische Psychologie und Fugendkunde (Germany)

168

BIBLIOGRAPHY

AEBLI, H. (1961) *Über die geistige Entwicklung des Kindes.* Stuttgart: Klett.
AEBLI, H. (1970) 'Piaget, and beyond', *Interchange*, 1, 12—24.
AHR, P.R., and YOUNISS, J. (1970) 'Reasons for failure on the class-inclusion problem', *Child Developm.*, 41, 131—43.
ALDRICH, B. (1970) 'A study of classification and Piaget's theory of concrete operations', *Diss. Abstr.*, 31, 2164—2165.
AMAIWA, S. (1973) 'A study of Piaget's concept of conservation', *Japan. J. Ed. Psych.*, 21, 1—11.
ANDERSON, R.C. (1965) 'Can first graders learn an advanced problem-solving skill?', *J. Ed. Psych.*, 56, 283—94.
ARMSTRONG, S., and MURRAY, F. (1975) 'Transitivity, conservation, necessity: the necessity of nonconservation'. Paper read at the Jean Piaget Society Meetings, Philadelphia.
AUSUBEL, D.P. (1965) 'Neobehaviourism and Piaget's views on thought and symbolic functioning', *Child Developm.*, 36, 1029—32.
AYERS, J.D., and HAUGEN, M. (1973) 'Measurement of training: an examination of method in conservation studies', *Can. J. Behav. Sc.*, 5, 67—75.
BANDURA, A., and HARRIS, M.B. (1966) 'Modification and syntactic style', *J. Exp. Child Psych.*, 4, 341—52.
BEARISON, D.J. (1969) 'Role of measurement operations in the acquisition of conservation', *Dev. Psych.*, 1, 653—60.
BEILIN, H. (1965) 'Learning and operational convergence in logical thought development', *J. Exp. Child Psych.*, 2, 317—39.
BEILIN, H. (1969) Cited in *The Role of Experience in the Rate and Sequence of Cognitive Development*, by M.L. Goldschmid. (Invited paper given at the Conference on Ordinal Scales of Cognitive Development, Monterey, California.).
BEILIN, H. (1971) 'The training and acquisition of logical operations'. In: ROSSKOPF, M.F, STEFFE, L.P. and TABACK, S. (Eds.), *Piagetian Cognitive-Developmental Research and Mathematical Education.* Washington, DC: National Council of Teachers of Mathematics.
BEILIN, H., KAGAN, J., and RABINOWITZ, R. (1966) 'Effects of verbal and perceptual training on water level representation', *Child Developm.*, 37, 317—29.
BERNDT, T.J., and WOOD, D.J. (1974) 'The development of time

concepts through conflict based on a primitive duration capacity', *Child Developm.*, 45, 825—28.

BERZONSKY, M.D., LOMARDO, T.P., and ONDRAKO, M.A. (1975) 'Changes in logical thinking as a function of induced disequilibrium', *J. Gen. Psych.*, 92, 255—60.

BINGHAM-NEWMAN, A.M., and HOOPER, F.H. (1974) 'Classification and seriation instruction and logical task performance in the preschool', *Am. Educ. Res. J.*, 11, 4, 379—93.

BIRCH, H.G., and BORTNER, M. (1966) 'Stimulus competition and category usage in normal children', *J. Gen. Psych.*, 109, 195—204.

BOLTON, N. (1975) Review of *Learning and the Development of Cognition*, by B. Inhelder, H. Sinclair and M. Bovet, London: Routledge and Kegan Paul. In: *The Durham Res. Rev.*, 7, 35, 1073—1074.

BOTVIN, G., and MURRAY, F.B. (in press) 'The efficacy of peer modeling and social conflict in the acquisition of conservation', *Child Developm.*

BOULANGER, F.D. (1974) 'The effects of instruction in the concept of speed and proportions on children in the third grade', *Diss. Abstr.*, 4479A—5379A (4686A) Xerox University Microfilms.

BRAINE, M.D.S. (1959) 'The ontogeny of certain logical operations: Piaget's formulations examined by non-verbal methods', *Psych. Mon. Gen. Appl.*, 73, No. 5. (whole No. 475).

BRAINE, M.D.S., and SHANKS, B.L. (1965a) 'The conservation of a shape property and a proposal about the origin of the conservations', *Can. J. Psych.*, 19, 197—207.

BRAINE, M.D.S., and SHANKS, B.L. (1965b) 'The development of conservation of size', *J. Verb. Learn. Behav.*, 4, 227—42.

BRAINERD, C.J. (1970) 'Continuity and discontinuity hypotheses in studies of conservation', *Dev. Psych.* 3, 225—8.

BRAINERD, C.J. (1973) 'Neo Piagetian training experiments revisited: Is there any support for the cognitive-developmental stage hypothesis', *Cogn.*, 2, 349—370.

BRAINERD, C.J. (1973a) 'Order of acquisition of transitivity, conservation, and class inclusion of length and height, *Dev. Psych.*, 8, 105—16.

BRAINERD, C.J. (1973b) 'Mathematical and behavioural foundations of number', *J. Gen. Psych.*, 88, 221—281.

BRAINERD, C.J. (1973c) 'Prologue to "The growth of the number concept"'. Unpublished manuscript, University of Alberta.

BRAINERD, C.J. (1974) 'Training and transfer of transitivity, conservation and class inclusion of length', *Child Developm.*, 45, 324—34.

BRAINERD, C.J., and ALLEN, T.W. (1971) 'Experimental inductions of the conservation of "first-order" quantitative invariants', *Psych. Bull.*, 75, 128—44.

BRAINERD, C.J., and ALLEN, T.W. (1971a) 'Training and generalization of density conservation: effects of feedback and consecutive similar stimuli', *Child Developm.*, 42, 693—704.

BRAINERD, C.J., and FRASER, M. (1973) 'A further test of the ordinal theory of number development'. Unpublished manuscript, University of Alberta, Alberta, Canada.

BRAINERD, C.J., and KASZOR, P. (1972) 'An analysis of performance hypotheses concerning children's class-inclusion reasoning errors'. Unpublished manuscript, Department of Psychology, University of Alberta, Edmonton.

BRISON, D.W. (1966) 'Acceleration of conservation of substance', *J. Gen. Psych.*, 109, 311—22.

BRISON, D.W., and BEREITER, C. (1967) 'Acquisition of conservation of substance in normal, retarded and gifted children'. In: BRISON, D.W. and SULLIVAN, E.V. (Eds.), *Recent Research on the Acquisition of Conservation of Substance*. Ontario Institute for Studies in Education, pp. 53—72.

BRODZINSKY, D., JACKSON, J., and OVERTON, W. (1972) 'Effects of perceptual shielding in the development of spatial perspectives', *Child Developm.*, 43, 1041—46.

BRUNER, J.S. (1960) *The Process of Education*. Cambridge, Mass: Harvard University Press.

BRUNER, J.S. (1964) 'The course of cognitive growth', *Am. Psych.*, 19, (1), 1—15.

BRUNER, J.S. (1966) *Toward a Theory of Instruction*. New York: W.W. Norton.

BRUNER, J.S., OLVER, R.R., and GREENFIELD, P.M. (1966) *Studies in Cognitive Growth*. New York: Wiley.

BRYANT, P.E. (1971) 'Cognitive development', *Brit. Med. Bull.*, 27, 3, 200—5.

BRYANT, P.E. (1972) 'The understanding of invariance by very young children', *Can. J. Psych.*, 26, 1, 78—95.

BRYANT, P.E. (1974) *Perception and Understanding in Young Children*. London: Methuen and Company Limited.

BUCHER, B., and SCHNEIDER, R.E. (1973) 'Acquisition and generalization of conservation by pre-schoolers, using operant training', *J. Exp. Child Psych.*, 16, 187—204.

BURKE, E. (1974) 'Training in logical thinking and its effects on the grouping strategies of eight-year-old children', *J. Child Psych. Psychiatr.*, 15, 303—12.

BURT, C. (1971) 'The development of training and reasoning', *Assoc. Ed. Psych. Newsletter.* 2, 10, 4—8.

CAMPBELL, D.T. and STANLEY, J.C. (1963) 'Experimental and quasi-experimental designs for research'. In: GAGE, N.L. (Ed.), *Handbook of Research on Teaching*. Chicago: Rand McNally, pp. 171—246.

CARLSON, J.S. *et al*. (1974) 'Der Effekt von Problemverbalisation bei verschiedenen Aufgabengruppen und Darbietungsformen des Raven Progressive Matrices Test', *Diagnostica.*, 20, 133—41.

CARLSON, J.S., and DILLON, R. (1976) 'Effects of testing conditions on Piaget Matrices and order of appearance problems: a study of competence VS performance'. Paper presented at the 6th international interdisciplinary seminar Piagetian theory and its implications for the helping professions, 30th January. Also personal communication.

CARUSO, J.L., and RESNICK, L.B. (1972) 'Task structure and transfer in children's learning of double classification skills', *Child Developm.*, 43, 1297—1308.

CHANDLER, M.J., GREENSPAN, S., and BARENBOIM, C. (1974) 'Assessment and training of role-taking and referential communication skills in institutionalized emotionally disturbed children', *Dev. Psych.*, 10, 4, 546—53.

CHISERI, M.J. (1975) 'Amenability to incorrect hypotheses in the extinction of conservation of weight in college students', *Merr.-Palm. Quart.*, 21, 2, 139—43.

CHRISTIE, J.F., and SMOTHERGILL, D.W. (1970) 'Discrimination and conservation of length', *Psychon. Sci.*, 21, 336—337.

CLARKE, A., CLARKE, A.D., and COOPER, G. (1970) 'The development of a set to perceive categorical relations'. In: HAYWOOD, H. (Ed.), *Social Cultural Aspects of Mental Retardation*. NY: Appleton-Century—Crofts.

COHEN, G.M. (1967) 'Conservation of quantity in children: the effect of vocabulary and participation', *Quart. Exp. Psych.*, 19, 150—4.

COX, M.V. (1976) 'The young child's representation of another's view', personal communication. Also PhD thesis, University of Hull.

COXFORD, A.F. (1964) 'The effects of instruction on stage placement in Piaget's seriation experiments', *Arith. Teach.*, 1, 4—9.

CURCIO, F., ROBBINS, O., and ELA, S.S. (1971) 'The role of body parts and readiness in acquisition of number conservation', *Child Developm.*, 42, 1641—6.

CURCIO, F., KATTEF, E., LEVINE, D., and ROBBINS, O. (1972) 'Compensation and susceptibility to conservation training', *Dev. Psych.*, 7, 259—65.

DANSET, A., and DUFOYER, J.P. (1968) 'Transitivité ou Inférence Prélogique Chez l'Enfant de Cinq Ans?', *Travaux & Documents de Lab. de Psychol. Génétique de Paris*, Sorbonne, III, No. 1.

DAVIDSON, T.E. (1975) 'The effects of drill on addition–subtraction fact learning: with implication of Piagetian reversibility', *Diss. Abstr.*, 36, 1, 1A–577A (p. 102–A).

DENNEY, D.R., and DENNEY, N.W. (1973) 'The use of classification for problem solving: a comparison of middle and old age', *Dev. Psych.*, 9, 275–78.

DENNEY, N.W., and ACITO, M.A. (1974) 'Classification training in two- and three-year-old children', *J. Exper. Child Psych.*, 17, 37–48.

DENNEY, N.W., and DENNEY, D.R. (1974) 'Modeling effects on the questioning strategies of the elderly', *Dev. Psych.*, 10, 3, 458.

EHRI, L.C., and MUZIO, I.M. (1974) 'Cognitive style and reasoning about speed', *J. Ed. Psych.*, 66, 4, 569–571.

ELKIND, D. (1964) 'Discrimination, seriation, and numeration of size and dimensional differences in young children: Piaget replication study VI', *J. Gen. Psych.*, 104, 275–96.

ELKIND, D. (1969) Cited in GOLDSCHMID, M.L. *The Role of Experience in the Rate and Sequence of Cognitive Development.* Invited paper presented at the conference on Ordinal Scales of Cognitive Development, Monterey, California.

ELLIS, L.G. (1972) The acquisition of Piagetian conservation by children in school – a training programme. Unpublished MEd thesis, University of Leicester. Also personal communication.

EMRICK, J.A. (1969) 'The acquisition and transfer of conservation skills by four year old children', *Diss. Abstr.*, 29, 2561.

ENNIS, R.H., FINKELSTEIN, M., SMITH, E., and WILSON, N. (1969) *Conditional Logic and Children.* Ithaca, New York: Cornell University, Cornell Critical Thinking Readiness Project, Phase II–C, Final Report.

FEIGENBAUM, K.D. (1971) 'A pilot investigation of the effects of training techniques designed to accelerate children's acquisition of conservation of discontinuous quantity', *J. Gen. Psych.*, 119, 13–23.

FEIGENBAUM, K.D. (1974) 'The relationship between concrete transitivity and social transitivity', *Psych. Mon.*, 5–42.

FESTINGER, L. (1957) *A Theory of Cognitive Dissonance.* Evanston, Illinois: Row, Peterson.

FIELD, D. (1974) 'Long-term effects of conservation training with ESN children', *J. Spec. Ed.*, 8, 3, 237–45.

FIGURELLI, J.C., and KELLER, H.R. (1972) 'The effects of training and socioeconomic class upon the acquisition of conservation concepts', *Child Developm.*, 43, 293–98.

FLANAGAN, J.C. (1958) *Flanagan Aptitude Classification Tests.* Chicago: Science Research Associates.

FLANDERS, J. (1968) 'A review of research on imitative behaviour',

Psych. Bull., 69, 316—37.
FLAVELL, J.H. (1963) The Developmental Psychology of Jean Piaget. Princeton: Van Nostrand.
FLAVELL, J.H., and WOHLWILL, J. (1969) 'Formal and functional aspects of cognitive development'. In: ELKIND, D. and FLAVELL, J. (Eds.), Studies in Cognitive Development: Essays in Honor of Jean Piaget. New York: Oxford University Press.
FOLEY, E.A. (1975) 'The effects of training in conservation of tonal and rhythmic patterns on second-grade children', Diss. Abstr., 35, 7, 3941A—4780A, (4584A)
FOURNIER, E. (1967) Un apprentissage de la Conservation des quantitiés continues par une technique d'Exercises opératoires. Unpublished doctoral dissertation, Montreal University.
FRANK, F. (1964) Cited by J.S. Bruner in 'The course of cognitive growth', Am. Psych., 19, 1—15.
FRANK, F. (1966) 'On the conservation of liquids'. In: BRUNER, J.S. et al., Studies in Cognitive Growth. New York: Wiley.
FREEBERG, N.E., and PAYNE, D.T. (1965) A Survey of Parental Practices Related to Cognitive Development in Young Children. Princeton, NJ: Inst. for Educ. Development.
FREEBERG, N.E., and PAYNE, D.T. (1967) 'Parental influence, on cognitive development in early childhood: a review', Child Developm., 38, 65—87.
FRIEDMAN, J., and PASNAK, R. (1973) 'Accelerated acquisition of classification skills by blind children', Dev. Psych., 9, 3, 333—37.
FURTH, H.G. (1970) Piaget for Teachers. Englewood Cliffs, New Jersey: Prentice Hall.
GAGNÉ, R.M. (1962) 'Military training and principles of learning', Am. Psych., 17, 83—91.
GAGNÉ, R.M. (1963) 'The learning requirements for inquiry', J. Res. Sci. Teach., 1, 144—53.
GAGNÉ, R.M. (1965) The Conditions of Learning. New York: Holt, Rinehart and Winston.
GAGNÉ, R.M. (1966) 'The learning of principles'. In: KLAUSMEIER, H.J., and HARRIS, C.W. (Ed.), Analysis of Concept Learning. New York: Academic Press.
GAGNÉ, R.M. (1968) 'Contributions of learning to human development', Psych. Rev., 75, 177—91.
GELMAN, R. (1967) Conservation, attention, and discrimination. Unpublished doctoral dissertation, University of California, Los Angeles.
GELMAN, R. (1969) 'Conservation acquisition: a problem of learning to attend to relevant attributes', J. Exper. Child Psych., 7, 167—87.
GHOLSON, B. and McCONVILLE, K. (1974) 'Effects of stimulus

differentiation training upon hypotheses, strategies and stereotypes in discrimination learning among kindergarten children', *J. Exper. Child Psych.*, 18, 81—97.

GHOLSON, B., O'CONNOR, J. and STERN, I. (1976) 'Hypothesis sampling systems among preoperational and concrete operational kindergarten children', *J. Exp. Child Psych.*, 21, 61—76.

GOLDSCHMID, M.L. (1969) 'The role of experience in the rate and sequence of cognitive development', invited paper given at the Conference on Ordinal Scales of Cognitive Development: Monterey, California: Feb. 9—11.

GOLDSCHMID, M.L. and BENTLER, P.M. (1968) 'The dimensions and measurement of conservation', *Child Developm.*, 39, 787—802.

GOLDSCHMID, M.L., and BENTLER, P.M. (1968b) *Manual: Concept Assessment Kit-Conservation.* San Diego, California: Educational and Industrial Testing Service.

GREENFIELD, P.M. (1966) 'On culture and conservation'. In: BRUNER, J.S. *et al.*, *Studies in Cognitive Growth.* New York: Wiley.

GREITZER, G., and JEFFREY, W.E. (1973) 'Negative effects of the pretest in training conservation of length', *Dev. Psych.*, 9, 3, 435.

GRIFFITHS, J.A., SHANTZ, C.U., and SIGEL, I.E. (1967) 'A methodological problem in conservation studies: the use of the relational terms', *Child Developm.*, 38, 841.

GRUEN, G.E. (1965) 'Experiences affecting the development of number conservation in children', *Child Developm.*, 36, 963—79.

GUTHKE, J. (1972) *Zur Diagnostik der intellektuellen Lernfahigkeit.* Berlin: Deutscher Verlag der Wissenschaften.

HALFORD, G.S. (1968) 'An experimental test of Piaget's notions concerning the conservation of quantity in children', *J. Exp. Child Psych.*, 6, 33—43.

HALFORD, G.S. (1969) 'An experimental analysis of the criteria used by children to judge quantities', *J. Exp. Child Psych.*, 8, 314—27.

HALFORD, G.S. (1971) 'Acquisition of conservation through learning a consistent classificatory system for quantities', *Aust. J. Psych.*, 23, 2, 151—9.

HALFORD, G.S., and FULLERTON, T.J. (1970) 'A discrimination task which induces conservation of number', *Child Developm.*, 41, 205—13.

HALL, V.C., and KINGSLEY, R.C. (1967) 'Problems in conservation research'. Paper read at Soc. Res. Child Developm., NY. March.

HALL, V.C., and KINGSLEY, R.C. (1968) 'Conservation and equilibration theory', *J. Gen. Psych.*, 113, 195—213.

HALL, V.C., and SIMPSON, G.J. (1968) 'Factors influencing extinction of weight conservation', *Merr.-Palm. Quart.*, 14, 197—210.

HAMEL, B.R. (1971) 'On the conservation of liquids', *Hum. Developm.*, 14, 39—46.

HAMEL, B.R. (1974) 'Piaget's number concept in first year school children', *Zeitschrift für Entwicklungspsychologie und Pädagogische Psychologie*, 6, 99—108.

HAMEL, B.R., and RIKSEN, B.O. (1973) 'Identity, reversibility, verbal rule instruction, and conservation', *Dev. Psych.*, 9, 1, 66—72.

HAMEL, B.R., VAN DER VEER, M.A.A., and WESTERHOF, R. (1972) 'Identity, language-activation training and conservation', *Brit. J. Ed. Psych.*, 42, 186—191.

HAMILTON, B.B. (1973) 'Control of the conservation response through discrimination learning set training for conserving and non-conserving transformations', *Diss. Abstr.*, 34, 4, 1407A—2071A (1700A), Xerox University Microfilms.

HAMMOND, K. (1966) 'Probabilistic functionalism: Egon Brunswick's integration of the history, theory and method of psychology'. In: HAMMOND, K. (Ed.), *The Psychology of Egon Brunswick*. New York: Holt, Rinehart and Winston, Inc.

HARRIS, M.L. (1974) 'Piagetian task performance as a function of training', *Diss. Abstr.*, 4479A—5379A (4869A), Xerox University Microfilms.

HATANO, G., and KUHARA, K. (1972) 'Training on class-inclusion problems', *Jap. Psych. Res.*, 14, 2, 61—9.

HOOPER, F.H. (1972) 'An evaluation of logical operations instruction in the preschool'. In: PARKER, R.K. (Ed.), *The Preschool in Action: Exploring Early Childhood Programmes*. Boston: Allyn and Bacon, pp. 134—186.

INHELDER, B. (1969) Cited in GOLDSCHMID, M. *Experience in the Rate and Sequence of Cognitive Development*. Invited paper given at the Conference in Ordinal Scales of Cognitive Development, Monterey, California, Feb. 9—11.

INHELDER, B. (1971) Comments on Goldschmid's Paper 'The Role of Experience in the Rate and Sequence of Cognitive Development and Measurement'. In: GREEN, D.R., FORD, M.P. and FLAMER, G.B. (Eds.), *Piaget and Measurement*. New York: McGraw Hill.

INHELDER, B., and PIAGET, J. (1964) *The Early Growth of Logic in the Child*. New York: Norton.

INHELDER, B., and SINCLAIR, H. (1969) 'Learning cognitive structures'. In: MUSSEN, P., LANGER, J., and COVINGTON, M. (Eds.), *Trends and Issues in Developmental Psychology*. New York: Holt, Rinehart and Winston.

INHELDER, B., SINCLAIR, H., and BOVET, M. (1974) *Learning and the Development of Cognition*. London: Routledge and Kegan Paul.

INHELDER, B., BOVET, M., SINCLAIR, H., and SMOCK, C.D. (1966)

'On cognitive development', *Am. Psych.*, 21, 1—23.

JACOBS, P.I. (1966) 'Programmed progressive matrices'. Proceedings of the 74th Annual Convention of the American Psychological Association, 2, 263—64, (Abstract).

JACOBS, P.I., and VANDEVENTER, M. (1968) 'Progressive matrices: an experimental, developmental, nonfactorial analysis', *Percep. Mot. Skills*, 27, 759—66.

JACOBS, P.I., and VANDEVENTER, M. (1969) 'Evaluating the teaching of intelligence', *Res. Bull.*, 69—20, Princeton, NJ: Educational Testing Service.

JACOBS, P.I., and VANDEVENTER, M. (1971) 'The learning and transfer of double-classification skills by first graders', *Child Developm.*, 42, 149—59.

JACOBS, P.I., and VANDEVENTER, M. (1971a) 'The learning and transfer of double-classification skills: a replication and extension', *J. Exp. Child Psych.*, 12, 240—57.

JAMMER, M. (1961) *Concepts of Mass in Classical and Modern Physics.* Cambridge: Harvard University Press.

JENSEN, J.A. (1969) 'Concrete transitivity of length: a method of assessment', *Bulletin Danish Inst. for Ed. Res.*, Copenhagen.

JOHNSON, M.L. (1974) 'The effects of instruction on length relations on the classification, seriation, and transitivity performance of first and second grade children', *J. Res. Maths. Educ.*, 5, 115—125.

KAPLAN, J.D. (1967) Teaching number conservation to disadvantaged children. Unpublished doctoral dissertation, Columbia University, New York.

KINGSLEY, R.C., and HALL, V.C. (1967) 'Training conservation through the use of learning sets', *Child Developm.*, 38, 1111—25.

KLAHR, D., and WALLACE, J.G. (1972) 'Class-inclusion processes'. In: FARNHAM-DIGGORY, S. (Ed.), *Information Processing in Children.* New York: Academic Press.

KLAUSMEIER, H.J., and HOOPER, F.H. (1974) 'Conceptual development and instruction'. In: CARROLL, J. (Ed.), *Review of Research in Education.* Hartsdale, NY.: American Educational Research Association.

KLEIN, N.K. (1974) 'Acquisition and retention of classification skills in the trainable mentally retarded', *Diss. Abstr.*, 34, 8, 4479A—5379A, (4928A), Xerox University Microfilms.

KNIGHT, C.A., and SCHOLNICK, E.F. (1973) 'Training comparison of the subset and the whole set; effects on inferences from negative instances', *Child Developm.*, 44, 162—165.

KOFSKY, E. (1966) 'A scalogram study of classificatory development', *Child Developm.*, 37, 1, 191—204.

KOHLBERG, L. (1968) 'Early education: a cognitive — developmental view', *Child Developm.*, 39, 1013—62.

KOHNSTAMM, G.A. (1963) 'An evaluation of part of Piaget's theory', *Acta Psychologie.*, 21, 313—56.

KOHNSTAMM, G.A. (1966) 'Experiments on teaching Piagetian thought operations'. Paper read at the Conference on Guided Learning Educational Research Council of Greater Cleveland.

KOHNSTAMM, G.A. (1967) *Piaget's Analysis of Class Inclusion, Right or Wrong?.* The Hague: Mouton.

KOHNSTAMM, G.A. (1967a) *Teaching Children to Solve a Piagetian Problem of Class Inclusion.* Amsterdam: Elsevier.

KOON, R.B. (1974) 'A study of the role of manipulatory grouping experience in the classification skill development of young children', *Diss. Abstr.*, 34, 10, 6171A—6792A, (6360A), Xerox University Microfilms.

KRAUSS, R.M., and GLUCKSBERG, S. (1969) 'The development of communication: competence as a function of age', *Child Developm.*, 40, 255—66.

KRAUSS, R.M., and WEINHEIMER, S. (1964) 'Changes in the length of reference phrases as a function of frequency of usage in social interaction: a preliminary study', *Psychonom. Sc.*, 1, 113—14.

KUHN, D. (1972) 'Mechanisms of change in the development of cognitive structures', *Child Developm.*, 43, 833—44.

KUHN, D. (1973) 'Imitation theory and research from a cognitive perspective', *Human Developm.*, 16, 157—80.

KUHN, D. (1974) 'Inducing development experimentally: comments on a research paradigm', *Dev. Psych.*, 10, 5, 596—600.

KUHN, D. and ANGELEV, J. (1975) 'An experimental study of the development of formal operational thought', personal communication. Unpublished study. Brief version presented at Society for Research in Child Development Convention, Denver, Colorado, April 10—13th.

LALLY, V.M. (1968) The effects of supplementary verbal stimulation on the development of concepts of number. DipEd thesis, Bristol University.

LANCASTER, R.P., and McMANIS, D.L. (1973) 'Training of number conservation in retardates', *Journ. Psych.*, 83, 303—313.

LANGER, J., and STRAUSS, S. (1972) 'Appearance, reality, and identity', *Cognit.*, 1. 105—128.

LEMERISE, T. (1974) 'Apprentissage de la notion de nombre par une methode fondée sur le modele piagetien de la fusion des classes et des relations', *Can. J. Behav. Sci.*, 6, 143—153.

LIFSCHITZ, M., and LANGFORD, P.E. (1975) 'Conservation: Transmitted or Constructed', personal communication.

LINDENBAUM, S., and BLUM, A. (1967) 'Development of concrete transitivity of length — empirical evidence for the debate'. Proc. 75th Ann. Conven. A.P.A., 165–166.

LISTER, C.M. (1969) 'The development of a concept of weight conservation in ESN children', *Brit. J. Ed. Psych.*, 245–52.

LISTER, C.M. (1970) 'The development of the concept of volume conservation in ESN children', *Brit. J. Ed. Psych.*, 40, 55–64.

LISTER, C.M. (1972) 'The development of ESN children's understanding of conservation in a range of attribute situations', *Brit. J. Ed. Psych.*, 42, 14–22.

LOVELL, K. (1969) Cited in 'The Role of Experience in the Rate and Sequence of Cognitive Development' by M. GOLDSCHMID. (Invited paper read at the Conference on Ordinal Scales of Cognitive Developm., Monterey, Calif., Feb. 9–11).

LOVELL, K. (1971) Comments on Goldschmid's Paper 'The Role of Experience in the Rate and Sequence of Cognitive Development'. In: GREEN, D.R., FORD, M.P., and FLAMER, G.B. (Eds.), *Piaget and Measurement*. New York: McGraw-Hill.

LOVELL, K., and OGILVIE, E. (1960) 'A study of the conservation of substance in the junior school child', *Brit. J. Ed. Psych.*, 30, 109–18.

MASON, J. (1969) A study of acceleration of concepts of number in young children through group treatment. MEd thesis, Bristol University.

MERMELSTEIN, E., and MEYER, E. (1968) 'Number Training Techniques and Their Effects on Different Populations'. Final Report. Contract No. OEO–1432, US Office of Economic Opportunity.

MERMELSTEIN, E., CARR, E., MILLS, D., and SCHWARTZ, J. (1967) 'Training techniques for the concept of conservation', *Alberta J. Ed. Psych.*, 13, 185–200, Project No. 6–8300.

MILLER, P.H. (1973) 'Attention to stimulus dimensions in the conservation of liquid quantity', *Child Developm.*, 44, 129–36.

MILLER, P.H., and HELDMEYER, K.H. (1975) 'Perceptual information in conservation: effects of screening', *Child Developm.*, 46, 588–92.

MILLER, P.H., HELDMEYER, K.H., and MILLER, S.A. (1975) 'Facilitation of conservation of number in young children', *Dev. Psych.*, 11, 2, 253.

MILLER, S.A. (1971) 'Extinction of conservation: a methodological and theoretical analysis', *Merr.-Palm. Quart.*, 319–34.

MILLER, S.A. (1973) 'Contradiction, surprise and cognitive change: the effect of disconfirmation of belief on conservers and non-conservers', *J. Exp. Child Psych.*, 15, 47–62.

MILLER, S.A., and BROWNELL, C. (1975) 'Peers, persuasion and

Piaget: dyadic interaction between conservers and nonconservers'. Paper read at Biennial meeting of Society for Research in Child Development, Denver.

MILLER, S.A., and LIPPS, L. (1973) 'Extinction of conservation and transitivity of weight', *J. Exper. Child Psych.*, 16, 388–402.

MILLER, S.A., SCHWARTZ, J., and STEWART, C. (1973) 'An attempt to extinguish conservation of weight in college students', *Dev. Psych.*, 8, 2, 316.

MINICHIELLO, M.D., and GOODNOW, J.J. (1969) 'Effect of an action cue on conservation of amount', *Psychonom. Sci.*, 16, 4, 200–1.

MODGIL, S. (1974) *Piagetian Research: A Handbook of Recent Studies.* Slough: NFER.

MONTADA, L. (1968) *Über die Funktion der Mobilität in der geistigen Entwicklung'.* Stuttgart: Klett.

MONTADA, L. (1970) *Die Lernpsychologie Jean Piaget.* Stuttgart: Klett.

MORI, I. (1973) 'On the formation of the concept of conservation in children', Japan. *J. Ed. Psych.*, 21, 32–42.

MURRAY, F.B. (1965) 'Conservation of illusion — distorted lengths and areas by primary school children', *J. Ed. Psych.*, 56, 62–6.

MURRAY, F.B. (1969) 'Conservation of mass, weight and volume in self and object', *Psych. Rep.*, 25, 941–42.

MURRAY, F.B. (1972) 'The acquisition of conservation through social interaction', *Dev. Psych.*, 6, 1–6.

MURRAY, F.B. (1976) 'Conservation deductions and ecological validity', personal communication. Also Paper presented at the meeting of the International Society for the Study of Behavioural Development, 1975.

MURRAY, F.B., and AMES, G. (1975) 'The acquisition of conservation through cognitive dissonance'. Paper read at the Biennial Meeting of Society for Research in Child Development, Denver.

MURRAY, F.B., and ARMSTRONG, S. (1975) 'A number conservation task on which children outperform adults'. Paper presented at the Jean Piaget Society, Philadelphia, Pa.

MURRAY, F.B., and HALDAS, J. (1974) 'Semantic aspects of conservation of weight transformations'. Paper read at Annual Meeting of Eastern Psychological Association, Philadelphia.

MURRAY, F.B., and HOLM, J. (1975) 'The absence of the continuity–discontinuity décalage'. Paper read at Annual Meeting of American Educational Research Association, Washington, DC.

MURRAY, F.B., and JOHNSON, P. (1969) 'Reversibility in the nonconservation of weight', *Psychonom. Sc.*, 16, 6, 285–86.

MURRAY, F.B., and JOHNSON, P. (in press) 'A curriculum model for the concept of weight', *J. Ed. Psych.*

MURRAY, F.B., and TYLER, J. (1975) 'Semantic characteristics of the conservation transformation'. Paper read at the Annual Meeting American Psychological Association, Chicago.

NUMMEDAL, S., and MURRAY, F.B. (1969) 'Conservation and connotative-denotative meaning', *Psychonom. Sc.*, 16, 6, 323—24.

OJEMANN, R.H., and PRITCHETT, K. (1963) 'Piaget and the role of guided experience in human development', *Percep. and Motor Skills*, 17, 927—40.

OKONJI, M.O. (1970) 'The Effect of Special Training on the Classificatory behaviour of Some Nigerian Ibo Children', *Brit. J. Ed. Psych.*, 40, 21—26.

OLMSTEAD, P., PARKS, C., and RICKEL, A. (1970) 'The development of classification skills in the preschool child', *Inter. Rev. of Educ.*, 16, 67—80.

OVERBECK, C., and SCHWARTZ, M. (1970) 'Training in conservation of weight', *J. Exp. Child Psych.*, 9, 253—64.

OVERTON, W. (1975) 'Environmental ontogeny: a cognitive view'. In: RIEGEL, K. and MEACHAM, J. (Eds.), *The Developing Individual in a Changing World*. The Hague: Mouton.

OVERTON, W., and BRODZINSKY, D. (1972) 'Perceptual and logical factors in the development of multiple classification', *Dev. Psych.*, 6, 104—109.

PARKER, R.K., RIEFF, M.L., and SPERR, S.J. (1971) 'Teaching multiple classification to young children', *Child Developm.*, 42, 1779—89.

PARKER, R.K., SPERR, S.J., and RIEFF, M.L. (1972) 'Multiple classification: A training approach', *Dev. Psych.*, 7, 2, 188—95.

PASCUAL-LEONE, J. (1970) 'A mathematical model for the transition rule in Piaget's developmental stages', *Acta Psych.*, 32, 301—45.

PEEL, E.A. (1968) 'Concrete learning and thinking'. In: LUNZER, E.A. and MORRIS, J.F. (eds.) *Development in Learning*. Volume II. London: Staples.

PIAGET, J. (1951) *The Psychology of Intelligence*. London: Routledge and Kegan Paul.

PIAGET, J. (1952) *The Origins of Intelligence in Children*. New York: Interm. Univses. Press.

PIAGET, J. (1952b) *The Child's Conception of Number*. New York: Humanities.

PIAGET, J. (1959) *Language and Thought of the Child*. London: Routledge and Kegan Paul.

PIAGET, J. (1964) 'Cognitive development in children: The Piaget Papers'. In: RIPPLE, R.E. and ROCKCASTLE, V.N. (Eds.), *Piaget Rediscovered, a report of the conference on cognitive studies and curriculum development*. Ithaca: School of Education, Cornell

University.

PIAGET, J. (1967) 'Cognitions and conservations: two views', *Contemp. Psycholog.*, 12, 532—33.

PIAGET, J. (1969) *The Child's Conception of Time*. London: Routledge and Kegan Paul.

PIAGET, J. (1972) 'Intellectual evolution from adolescence to adulthood', *Human Developm.*, 15, 1—12.

PIAGET, J. (1974) 'Foreword'. In: INHELDER, B., SINCLAIR, H. and BOVET, M. *Learning and the Development of Cognition*. London: Routledge and Kegan Paul.

PIAGET, J., and INHELDER, B. (1941) *Le Développement des Quantités chez l'Enfant*. Paris: Delachaux et Niestlé.

PIAGET, J., and INHELDER, B. (1956) *The Child's Conception of Space*. London: Routledge and Kegan Paul.

PIAGET, J., and INHELDER, B. (1969) *The Psychology of the Child*. London: Routledge and Kegan Paul.

PIAGET, J., INHELDER, B. (1971) *Mental Imagery in the Child*. New York: Basic Books.

PIAGET, J., INHELDER, B., and SZEMINSKA, A. (1960) *The Child's Conception of Geometry*. London: Routledge and Kegan Paul.

PINARD, A., and LAURENDEAU, M. (1969) '"Stage" in Piaget's cognitive-developmental theory: Exegesis of a concept'. In: ELKIND, D and FLAVELL, J.H. (Eds.), *Studies in Cognitive Development*. New York: Oxford University Press.

PUFALL, P.B. (1973) 'Induction of linear-order concepts: a comparison of three training techniques', *Child Developm.*, 44, 642—45.

RATTAN, M.S. (1974) 'The role of language, manipulation and demonstration in the acquisition, retention, and transfer of conservation', *Alberta J. Ed. Res.*, 20, 217—25.

RESNICK, L.B. (1967) 'Design of an early learning curriculum'. Working Paper 16., Pittsburgh: Learning Research and Development Center, University of Pittsburgh.

RIEGEL, K. (1975) 'From traits and equilibrium toward developmental dialectics'. Paper read at the Nebraska Symposium on Motivation.

ROBERGE, J.J. (1971) 'An analysis of response patterns for conditional reasoning schemes', *Psych. Sci.*, 22, 338—39.

ROLL, S. (1970) 'Reversibility training and stimulus desirability as factors in conservation of number', *Child Developm.*, 501—7.

ROSENTHAL, T.L., and ZIMMERMAN, B.J. (1972) 'Modeling by exemplification and instruction in training conservation', *Dev. Psych.*, 6, 3, 392—401.

ROTHENBERG, B.B. (1969) 'Conservation of number among four and five-year-old children: some methodological considerations', *Child Developm.*, 40, 383—406.

ROTHENBERG, B.B., and OROST, J.H. (1969) 'The training of conservation of number in young children', *Child Developm.*, 40, 707–26.

SAWADA, D., and NELSON, L.D. (1967) 'Conservation of length and the teaching of linear measurement: a methodological critique', *Arithmetic Teacher*, 14, 345–8.

SCHMALOHR, E., and WINKELMANN, W. (1969) *Zeitschrift f. Entwicklungspsychologie u. Pädagogische Psychologie*, Band. I, Heft, 2, 5, 93–102.

SEILER, B.Th. (1968) *Die Reversibilität in der Entwicklung des Denkens*. Stuttgart: Klett.

SHANTZ, C.U., and SIGEL, I. (1967) 'Logical operations and concepts of conservation in children: a training study'. Center for Developmental Studies in Cognition, The Merrill-Palmer Institute, Detroit, Michigan.

SHANTZ, C.U., and WILSON, K.E. (1972) 'Training communication skills in young children', *Child Developm.*, 43, 693–98.

SHEPPARD, J.L. (1973) 'Conservation of part and whole in the acquisition of class inclusion', *Child Developm.*, 44, 380–83.

SHEPPARD, J.L. (1974) 'Compensation and combinatory systems in the acquisition and generalization of conservation', *Child Developm.*, 45, 717–30.

SHEPPARD, J.L. (1974a) 'The child's concept of horizontality with water levels: a training study', *Aust. J. Psych.*, 26, 3, 191–98.

SHEPPARD, J.L. (1974b) 'Concrete operational thought and developmental aspects of solutions to a task based on a mathematical three-group', *Dev. Psych.*, 10, 116–23.

SIEGEL, S. (1956) *Non-parametric Statistics*. New York: Wiley.

SIEGLER, R.S., and LIEBERT, R.M. (1972) 'Effects of presenting relevant rules and complete feedback on the conservation of liquid quantity', *Dev. Psych.*, 7, 2, 133–9.

SIGEL, I.E. (1964) 'The attainment of concepts'. In: HOFFMAN, M.L., and HOFFMAN, L.V. (Ed.), *Review of Child Development Research*. Volume I. New York: Russell Sage Foundation.

SIGEL, I.E. (1966) *Child Development and Social Science Education*. Part 4, A teaching strategy derived from some Piagetian concepts, Detroit: Merrill-Palmer Institute.

SIGEL, I.E., and OLMSTEAD, P. (1970) 'Modification of cognitive skills among lower-class Black children'. In: HELLMUTH, J. (Ed.), *Disadvantaged Children*. Volume 3, 'Compensating Education: a National Debate'. New York: Brunner / Mazel Publishers, pp. 300–38.

SIGEL, I.E., ANDERSON, L.M., and SHAPIRO, M. (1966) 'Categorization behaviour of lower- and middle-class Negro preschool children: differences in dealing with representation of familiar objects', *J. Negro Educ., Summer,* 218—229.

SIGEL, I.E., ROEPER, A., and HOOPER, F.H. (1966) 'A training procedure for the acquisition of Piaget's conservation of quantity: a pilot study and its replication', *Brit. J. Ed. Psych.,* 36, 301—11.

SILVERMAN, I.W., and GEIRINGER, E. (1973) 'Dyadic interaction and conservation induction: a test of Piaget's equilibration model', *Child Developm.,* 44, 815—20.

SILVERMAN, I.W., and STONE, J. (1972) 'Modifying cognitive functioning through participation in a problem-solving group', *J. Ed. Psych.,* 63, 603—608.

SIMCOX, N.M. (1970) 'Improvement in the logic of eight-year-old children', *Ed. Rev.,* 23, 69—77.

SINCLAIR, H. (1969) 'Developmental psycholinguistics'. In: EL- KIND, D. and FLAVELL, J.H. (Eds.), *Studies in Cognitive Development: essays in honour of Jean Piaget.* New York: Oxford University Press, pp. 315—336.

SMEDSLUND, J. (1961) 'The acquisition of conservation of substance and weight in children: an attempt to extinguish visual components of the weight concept', *Scan. J. Psych.,* 2, 153—55.

SMEDSLUND, J. (1961a) 'The acquisition of conservation of substance and weight in children: II, External reinforcement of conservation of the weight and of the operations of addition and subtraction', *Scan. J. Psych.,* 2, 71—84.

SMEDSLUND, J. (1962) 'The acquisition of conservation of substance and weight in children: VII: conservation of discontinuous quantity and the operations of adding and taking away', *Scan. J. Psych.,* 3, 69—77.

SMEDSLUND, J. (1963) 'The effects of observation on children's representation of the spatial orientation of a water surface', *J. Gen. Psych.,* 102, 195—201.

SMEDSLUND, J. (1963a) 'Patterns of experience and the acquisition of conservation of length', *Scan. J. Psych.,* 4, 257—64.

SMEDSLUND, J. (1965) 'The development of transitivity of length: a comment on Braines reply', *Child Developm.,* 36, 577—80.

SMEDSLUND, J. (1966) 'Microanalysis of concrete reasoning: I, The difficulty of some combinations of addition and subtraction of one unit', *Scan. J. Psych.,* 7, 145—67.

SMEDSLUND, J. (1968) 'Conservation and resistance to extinction: a comment on Hall and Simpson's article', *Merr. — Palm. Quart.,* 14, 3.

SMEDSLUND, J. (1969) 'Psychological diagnostics', *Psych Bull.,* 71, 237—48.

SMITH, I.D. (1968) 'Effects of training procedures upon the acquisition of conservation of weight', *Child Developm.*, 39, 515–26.

SONSTROEM, A.M. (1966) 'On the conservation of solids'. In: BRUNER, J.S., OLVER, R.R. and GREENFIELD, P.M. *et al.* (Eds.), *Studies in Cognitive Growth*. New York: Wiley.

STEINER, G. (1974) 'On the psychological reality of cognitive structures: a tentative synthesis of Piaget's and Bruner's theories', *Child Developm.*, 45, 891–99.

STRAUSS, S. (1972) 'Inducing cognitive development and learning: a review of short-term training experiments 1: the organismic development approach, *Cognition*, 1, 4, 329–57.

STRAUSS, S. (1972a) 'Learning theories of Gagné and Piaget: Implications for curriculum development', *Teachers' College Record*, 74, 1, 81–102.

STRAUSS, S. (1974) 'A reply to Brainerd', *Cogn.*, 3, 2, 155–185.

STRAUSS, S., and ILAN, J. (in press) 'Length conservation and speed: organizational disequilibrium training between concepts', *J. Ed. Psych.*

STRAUSS, S., and LANGER, J. (1970) 'Operational thought inducement', *Child Developm.*, 41, 163–75.

STRAUSS, S., and RIMALT, T.I. (1974) 'Effects of organizational disequilibrium training on structural elaboration', *Dev. Psych.*, 10, 4, 526–33.

STRAUSS, S., DANZIGER, Y., and RAMATI, T. (1974) 'College students' understanding of possible violation of physical laws of conservation of mass, weight, operating of the lever, and gravity', Tel-Aviv University, Unpublished manuscript.

SULLIVAN, E.V. (1967) 'Acquisition of conservation of substance through film modeling techniques'. In: BRISON, D.W. and SULLIVAN, E.V. (Eds.), *Recent Research on the Acquisition of Conservation of Substance*. Ontario Institute for Studies in Education, pp. 11–23.

SULLIVAN, E.V. (1969) 'Transition problems in conservation research', *J. Gen. Psych.*, 115, 41–54.

SVENDSEN, D. (1973) 'Verbal training and development of concrete operations in adult mental retardates'. Paper presented at the second Prague Conference with International Participation, Psychology of Human Learning and Problem Solving, July 16–20. Also personal communication.

WAGHORN, L., and SULLIVAN, E.V. (1970) 'The exploration of transition rules in conservation of quantity (substance) using film mediated modeling', *Acta. Psychol.*, 32, 65–80.

WALLACE, J.G. (1965) *Concept Growth and Education of the Child.*

Slough: NFER.

WALLACE, J.G. (1967) An inquiry into the development of concepts of number in young children involving a comparison of verbal and non-verbal methods of assessment and acceleration. PhD thesis, Bristol University.

WALLACE, J.G. (1972) *Stages and Transition in Conceptual Development*. Slough: NFER.

WALLACH, L. (1969) 'On the bases of conservation'. In: ELKIND, D. and FLAVELL, J.H. (Eds.), *Studies in Cognitive Development*, pp. 191—219. London: Oxford University Press.

WALLACH, L., and SPROTT, R.L. (1964) 'Inducing number-conservation in children', *Child Developm.*, 35, 1057—71.

WALLACH, L., WALL, J.A., and ANDERSON, L. (1967) 'Number conservation: the roles of reversibility, addition—subtraction, and misleading perceptual cues', *Child Developm.*, 38, 425—42.

WASON, P., and JOHNSON-LAIRD, P. (1972) *Psychology of Reasoning: Structures and Content*. Cambridge, Mass: Harvard University Press.

WEINREB, N., and BRAINERD, C.J. (1975) 'A developmental study of Piaget's groupement model of the emergence of speed and time concepts', *Child Developm.*, 46, 176—185.

WHITEMAN, M., and PEISACH, E. (1970) 'Perceptual and sensori-motor supports for conservation tasks', *Dev. Psych.*, 2, 2, 247—56.

WINER, G. (1968) 'Induced set and acquisition of number conservation', *Child Developm.*, 39, 195—205.

WINKELMANN, W. (1975) *Test zur Erfassung kognitiver Operationen*. Braunschweig: Westerman.

WOHLWILL, J.F. (1968) 'Responses to class-inclusion questions with verbally and pictorially presented items', *Child Developm.*, 39, 449—65.

WOHLWILL, J.F. (1970) 'The place of structured experience in early cognitive development', *Interchange.*, 1, 13—27.

WOHLWILL, J.F., and LOWE, R.C. (1962) 'Analysis of the development of the conservation of number', *Child Developm.*, 33, 153—67.

YOUNISS, J., and MURRAY, J.P. (1970) 'Transitive inference with non-transitive solutions controlled', *Dev. Psych.*, 2, 169—175.

ZIEGENFUSS, P.L. (1973) 'Development and training of time concepts in young children', *Diss. Abstr.*, 33, 10, 5343A—5882A (5420A), Xerox University Microfilms.

ZIGLER, E., and BUTTERFIELD, E.C. (1968) 'Motivation aspects of changes in IQ test performance of culturally deprived nursery school children', *Child Developm.*, 39, 1—14.

ZIMILES, H. (1963) 'A note on Piaget's concept of conservation', *Child Developm.*, 34, 691—95.

ZIMMERMAN, B.J. (1974) 'Modification of young children's grouping
    strategies: the effects of modeling, verbalization, incentives, and
    age', *Child Developm.*, 45, 1032—41.
ZIMMERMAN, B.J., and ROSENTHAL, T.L. (1974) 'Conserving and
    retaining equalities and inequalities through observation and
    correlation', *Dev. Psych.*, 10, 2, 260—68.

INDEX

Acito, M.A., 75
Aebli, H., 70, 71, 93
Ahr, P.R., 63
Aldrich, B., 64
Allen, T.W., 38, 72, 129
Amaiwa, S., 37
Ames, G., 144
Anderson, L.M., 65, 126
Anderson, R.C., 27, 28, 63, 65, 109, 126
Angelev, J., 72, 73
Armstrong, S., 140, 142
Ayers, J.D., 33

Bandura, A., 148
Barenboim, C., 78, 103, 104
Bearison, D.J., 150
Beilin, H., 18, 29, 31, 41, 42, 45, 46, 57, 58, 63, 68, 72, 74, 75, 80, 93, 116, 118, 121
Bentler, P.M., 18, 78, 122, 124, 146, 161, 162
Bereiter, C., 136
Berndt, T.J., 61, 85
Berzonsky, M.D., 73, 86
Bingham-Newman, A.M., 67, 87
Birch, H.G., 93
Blum, A., 53
Bolton, N., 84
Bortner, M., 93
Botkin, P.A., 104
Botvin, G., 39, 144
Boulanger, F.D., 61, 88
Bovet, M., 72, 81, 84, 93, 117
Braine, M.D.S., 28, 52
Brainerd, C.J., 22, 23, 31, 32, 33, 38, 60, 68, 72, 73, 89, 90, 129, 154, 155, 156, 158
Brison, D.W., 42, 136, 137
Brodzinsky, D., 49, 93
Brownell, C., 20, 39, 143
Bruner, J.S., 17, 36, 41, 42, 66, 84, 92, 110, 121, 150
Brunswick, E., 142
Bryant, P.E., 30, 54, 63, 84
Bucher, B., 28, 34, 90, 91
Burke, E., 66, 91, 92

Burt, C., 63
Butterfield, E.C., 79

Campbell, D.T., 87
Carlson, J.S., 71, 72, 92, 94
Carr, E., 42
Caruso, J.L., 46, 67, 102, 103
Chandler, M.J., 78, 103, 104
Chiseri, M.J., 21, 104
Christie, J.F., 50
Clarke, A., 93
Clarke, A.D., 93
Cohen, G.M., 48
Cooper, G., 93
Cowan, P.A., 104
Cox, M.V., 59, 105
Coxford, A.F., 87
Curcio, F., 30, 31

Danset, A., 52, 53
Danziger, Y., 22, 155
Davidson, T.E., 39, 106
Denney, D.R., 77
Denney, N.W., 75, 77
Dillon, R., 71, 72, 92
Dolinsky, H., 101
Dufoyer, J.P., 52, 53
Dunn, L.M., 116, 145

Ehri, L.C., 62, 107
Ela, S.S., 30, 31
Elkind, D., 18, 87
Ellis, L.G., 70, 108
Emrick, J.A., 50
Ennis, R.H., 63

Feigenbaum, K.D., 31, 53
Festinger, L., 41
Field, D., 29, 47, 115
Figurelli, J.C., 29
Flamer, G.B., 80
Flanagan, J.C., 108
Flanders, J., 75
Flavell, J.H., 39, 93, 103, 118, 143, 149
Foley, E.A., 37, 117
Ford, M.P., 80